AN INTRODUCTION TO TUDOR DRAMA

Publius Cornelius and Gaius Flaminius, rival suitors for the hand of Lucres, daughter of the Senator, Fulgens

From an illustrated MS. in the Bibliothèque Royale, Brussels, of Jean Mielot's French version of the source of H. Medwall's *Fulgens and Lucres*

AN INTRODUCTION TO TUDOR DRAMA

BY

FREDERICK S. BOAS

M.A. (OXON.); HON. LL.D. (ST. ANDREWS)

GREENWOOD PRESS, PUBLISHERS
WESTPORT, CONNECTICUT

Library of Congress Cataloging in Publication Data

Boas, Frederick Samuel, 1862-1957.
An introduction to Tudor drama.

Reprint of the 1933 ed. published by Oxford at the Clarendon Press, Oxford, Eng.
Includes index.
1. English drama--Early modern and Elizabethan, 1500-1700--History and criticism. I. Title.
PR646.B6 1977 822'.2'09 76-50079
ISBN 0-8371-9073-8

Originally published in 1933 by Oxford at the Clarendon Press

This reprint has been authorized by the Clarendon Press Oxford

Reprinted in 1977 by Greenwood Press, Inc.

Library of Congress Catalog Card Number 76-50079

ISBN 0-8371-9073-8

Printed in the United States of America

PREFACE

It has been thought well that my *Introduction to the Reading of Shakespeare*, issued as one of the World's Manuals in 1927, should be followed by an *Introduction to Tudor Drama*. This volume, though planned on kindred lines, has a somewhat wider range, and appears in a different form. Its aim is to stimulate and broaden the interest in Tudor plays and playwrights. Attention has been concentrated on these, and only incidental reference has been made to stage-history.

I have endeavoured to set forth briefly the broad results of recent research and criticism, e.g. on Medwall and Rastell, Bale and Udall, Munday and Marlowe. But in a book of this scope it has not, as a rule, been possible to cite authorities, or discuss disputed points.

The term 'Tudor' has been strictly interpreted, and I have therefore not included playwrights like Ben Jonson and Chapman, whose main achievement lies in the Stuart period. Sixteenth-century drama provides abundant and ever-increasing avenues for study.

In quotations from plays acted before 1580, and from those like *King Johan* and *Sir Thomas More*, which are extant only in manuscript, I have used the original spelling. In the case of the later dramatists, from Lyly and Kyd onwards, who come within the Shakespearian circle, the spelling has been modernized. The comparison may be of some help and interest to students.

I am indebted to the officials of the Clarendon Press for their help in the selection of illustrations. I have to thank Professor A. W. Reed (co-editor with me of *Fulgens and Lucres*) and Messrs. George Routledge & Sons for permitting me to reproduce the frontispiece to this volume, which first appeared as an illustration of an article by Dr. Reed in a volume on *Chivalry*; also the authorities of the Henry E. Huntington Library, San Marino, California, and Dr. W. W. Greg, the Malone Society General Editor, for similar permission in the case of the facsimile from Bale's *King Johan*.

It is a pleasure to be allowed to link this book, as a grateful tribute, with the name of Sir Barry Jackson, who at the Malvern Theatrical Festivals is so successfully renewing the stage-life of our older plays. At his call *Wether* and *Ralph Roister Doister*, *The Alchemist*, and *A Woman Killed by Kindness*, have proved that they are more than 'period' plays, and that they can still in a twentieth-century theatre move our laughter or our tears.

F. S. B.

March, 1933.

CONTENTS

LIST OF ILLUSTRATIONS

I

THE EARLY TUDOR GROUP OF PLAYWRIGHTS

IN my *Introduction to the Reading of Shakespeare* I have given some suggestions to those who are beginning the study of Shakespeare's plays and poems and I have indicated what are likely to be helpful lines of approach to them. The question has been asked:

> What does he know of England
> Who only England knows?

So, in a measure, it is with England's master-dramatist. He does not stand alone in isolated majesty. His work is the climax, the consummation of the efforts and achievements of forerunners for a century before he began to write. Unless we know something of what they were and did, of what they contributed to the English stage before Shakespeare came both to crown and to eclipse what they had so far accomplished, we shall not be able to see his own work in its true proportion and perspective. Some knowledge of predecessors and contemporaries in the field of drama is therefore necessary to every reader of Shakespeare after he has become more or less familiar with the plays preserved in the First Folio of 1623.

This is alone a sufficient reason for the study of early Tudor drama. But that study is also an end in itself. We understand Shakespeare all the better if we have made acquaintance with Medwall and Heywood, Lyly and Greene, Kyd and Marlowe, and with school and university playwrights. But these would be well worth our attention, and would more than repay our pains in reading them if Shakespeare had never written a line.

I have spoken of him as having forerunners for a century. But from some points of view they go back much further; and are to be found in the unknown writers of the great cycles of religious plays (*Miracles*), followed by the series of allegorical plays (*Moralities*) of which *Everyman* is the best known. The *Miracles* and *Moralities* kept up a continuous dramatic tradition in England from the beginning of the fourteenth century or before, and habituated the townsfolk whether as actors or spectators to theatrical performances. Echoes of these performances are heard in the plays of Shakespeare and his fellows, and *Moralities*, as will be seen, continued to be written during the sixteenth century. But in its essential spirit Tudor drama was secular, and it is therefore from the beginnings of secular drama in England that this short survey may take its start.

It is fortunate for those entering upon the study of our present subject that on no period of theatrical history has more fresh light been recently thrown than on the two first Tudor reigns. The traditional view has been that English tragedy and comedy both took their rise under the influence of the classical drama or, more strictly speaking, the Latin drama of Seneca, Plautus, and Terence. It is true that this influence, as we shall see, was great and in many ways beneficial. But it has now been made clear that in the early Tudor era there was a group of playwrights who, though scholarly and showing the stamp of the new learning, formed what may be truly called a native English dramatic school. They were indebted to foreign sources for part of their material, but their technique and methods of characterization were their own.

It is remarkable that all the members of this group were related to, or associated with, the most illustrious figure of the earlier days of the English Renaissance, Sir Thomas More. He was himself, according to the evidence of his contemporary, John Bale, a writer of comedies in his youth, though we cannot with certainty identify any of these. We are also told by his son-in-law, William Roper, that when he was a page in the household of Cardinal Morton he was an amateur actor. He would 'sodenly sometymes slip in among the players and make a parte of his owne there presently among them'. In Morton's service he doubtless came into touch with Henry Medwall, the Cardinal's chaplain, and author of our first known secular play, *Fulgens and Lucres*. This play was printed by John Rastell, himself a dramatist, who married More's sister, Elizabeth. Their daughter, Joan, married John Heywood, the leading dramatist of the group. Thus Tudor drama begins as almost a family affair, with the genial, finely-tempered spirit of More presiding over it.

It is only by a happy accident that we are able to realize the importance of Henry Medwall as the first of our Tudor playwrights. Except for some details about his clerical career between 1490 and 1501 we know little about his life. It is from the title-pages of his two plays that we learn that he was Morton's chaplain. Of each of these only one copy (so far as is known) has survived. The copy of *Nature* is in the British Museum; that of *Fulgens and Lucres*, which came to light in 1919, is now in the Huntington Library in California. *Nature*, though it shows the influence of the new learning, and has episodes of realistic humour, belongs to the *Morality* class. It is an allegorical play, in two parts, dealing with the temptations to which Man, the central figure, is subjected before he finally repents and is received into grace. It is one of the best of its type and can still be read with enjoyment, but the day of that type was passing. In *Fulgens and Lucres*, on the other hand, Medwall looks not back but forward and gives us a play neither biblical nor allegorical, but introducing representative figures from the lay world. Allusions in the play itself show that it was acted in the great hall of a lord's house, probably Morton's palace at Lambeth. We get a vivid picture of the actors in their gay costumes entering the hall where the owner has already provided good cheer, and where he will further entertain his guests to dinner between the two parts of the play. There is some reason for believing that these guests included the Spanish and Flemish ambassadors and that *Fulgens and Lucres* was performed about Christmas 1497.

Its plot is taken from a treatise, *De Vera Nobilitate*, a short piece of fiction, with a moral aim, by an Italian humanist, Bonaccorso. This told how Fulgentius, a Roman Senator, had a beautiful and wise daughter Lucretia, who was wooed by Publius Cornelius, a rich pleasure-loving aristocrat, and by Gaius Flaminius, a virtuous man of humble birth. Lucretia refers them to her father, who in his turn appeals to the Senate for a decision which, after speeches by the suitors, is finally withheld. This Latin treatise became extremely popular, and was translated into French by Jean Mielot and afterwards into English. The English version was by a prominent Yorkist nobleman, John Tiptoft, Earl of Worcester, and was printed by William Caxton. It was this that Medwall used, but in turning the story into a play he made important changes. Instead of leaving the decision between the two suitors 'in the air', he makes Lucres (as he anglicizes her name) herself choose the poor but virtuous wooer. This is both theatrically more effective, and implied at that period real moral courage. Medwall's Lucres is more fortunate than Shakespeare's Portia in that she has not to depend for a husband on the luck of the caskets, but is free to make her own choice. Yet she foreshadows Shakespeare's heroine in her dutifulness, her lawyer-like gifts of advocacy, and her insight into the characters of those who seek her hand. And there is another way in which Medwall anticipates Shakespeare. He added to the original story a comic underplot in which the servants of the two suitors for Lucres are rivals for the favours of her handmaid. It may not be more than amusing 'knock-about' farce, good of its kind, but in its primitive way it is born of the same sure dramatic instinct that added the wit-combats of Benedick and Beatrice to the troubled love-story of Hero and Claudio, and the scenes in the Boar's Head Tavern to those in the council-room or on the battle-field in *King Henry IV*. And if Medwall did not vary from verse to prose, he used the seven-lined rhyme royal stanza for serious purposes and a lighter form of stanza elsewhere.

John Rastell, the printer of *Fulgens and Lucres*, was a man of many occupations and interests. Born probably about 1475, he was a member of a long-established Coventry family. He was educated for the law, probably at the Middle Temple. He was married to Elizabeth, sister of Sir Thomas More, before 1504, and lived for a number of years in his native town, which had been one of the chief medieval centres for plays and pageants. In the French war of 1512–14 he did transport service, and in 1517 he set off from Greenwich in a ship called the *Barbara* on a voyage to the new-found lands across the Atlantic. This ended abruptly (but, as will be seen, fortunately for us) at Waterford.

Meanwhile he had set up as a printer in St. Paul's Churchyard, and eventually owned three shops in different quarters. In this business he was helped by his son, William. The printing of law-books was a special feature of the Rastell press, but it also issued histories, pamphlets, and plays.

In 1529 he was a member of the Reformation Parliament, and henceforward he became increasingly associated with the Lutheran movement, in the opposite camp to that of his brother-in-law. He acted as an agent to Thomas Cromwell, who however did little on his behalf, and did not save him from imprisonment for opposition to a Royal proclamation of 1535. He was still in confinement when he died on 25 June 1536.

Among these manifold pre-occupations Rastell had found time to take an active part in the production of pageants and plays. He devised the magnificently ornamented roofs of the Banqueting Hall for the Field of the Cloth of Gold at Guisnes in 1520. In the summer of 1522 when Henry VIII and the Emperor Charles V went to St. Paul's he erected a pageant at 'the Lyttyl Conduit by Paul's Gate'. According to the chronicler, Halle:

> There was buylded a place like heaven, curiously painted with cloudes, orbes,[1] starres and the Ierarchies of angels. In the top of this pagiant was a great type,[2] and out of this type sodainly issued out of a cloude a fayre lady richely apparelled, and then al the minstrels whiche wer in the pagiant played, and the angels sang, and sodainly againe

[1] Printed 'erbes'. [2] A cupola or dome.

she was assumpted into the cloud, whiche was very curiously done, and aboute this pagiant stode the Apostles.

In 1527 when ambassadors from France came to arrange a marriage with Princess Mary, there was an entertainment at Greenwich, for which Holbein painted a picture of the 'Taking of Terouenne', and Rastell devised an astronomical pageant 'The Father of Heaven'. He also (as we know from a lawsuit between him and the carpenter, Henry Walton) had a stage erected in the grounds of a house which he built after 1524 in Finsbury Fields. His wife and a tailor had made costumes for the players, which Rastell had lent to Walton during a lengthy visit to France, and which the latter failed to return, after hiring them out to actors of stage-plays and interludes.

It is to be presumed, though there is no documentary record, that Rastell's plays, or some of them, were performed on his own stage. No play bears his name on the title-page: his authorship rests on circumstantial, but cogent, evidence. He wrote and published various books in prose, including an historical work, *The Pastyme of People*, and a controversial treatise *The Boke of Purgatory*, both containing very distinctive personal views. When we find these views repeated in plays of which Rastell was the publisher, it may reasonably be concluded that the plays are from his pen. Thus in the *Pastyme of People* he asserts that judges and other legal officers should be removable every few years. At the end of 'a dyaloge . . . compilid in maner of an enterlude with diuers toys and gestis addyt therto', entitled of *Gentleness and Nobility*, and published by Rastell, the same view is emphasized. Again, in his *Boke of Purgatory* he appeals to 'natural reason and good philosophy' instead of to scriptural authority. A similar attitude, very unusual at the time, is adopted by the speaker in *Gentleness and Nobility* who is most representative of Rastell.

The speakers are three, a merchant, a knight, and a ploughman, debating who is a very gentleman and who is a nobleman. The subject of discussion and the addition of 'toys and gestis' carry us back to *Fulgens and Lucres*, by which Rastell was doubtless influenced. He lacked, however, Medwall's gifts for characterization and plot-construction. The strong points of the interlude are the raciness of the dialogue and the sustained level of the argument. The merchant, in opposition to the knight who is proud of his descent, declares that he is a gentleman

> that gentilly
> Doth gyf unto other men lovyngly
> Such thing as he hath of his own proper.

He proceeds to enlarge, in curiously modern fashion, on his services to the commonwealth by his importing of necessary commodities from abroad. But the ploughman maintains (as Rastell does also in the *Boke of Purgatory*) that the noblest thing is that which is most independent, and that therefore he is the noblest man, as by ploughing and tilling the ground he satisfies his own needs and those of others. And from this the debate proceeds again in Part II to more modern problems of the rights of property and inheritance.

The evidence of Rastell's authorship of the *Interlude of the Four Elements* is found not only in parallels with his prose works but in an autobiographical passage referring to the mutiny of the mariners that cut short his expedition in 1517 to the new-found lands. It was not difficult to introduce this personal reminiscence for the interlude is very much of a treatise on cosmology, astronomy, and geography, on which subjects the characters give each other lectures. All these characters are personifications—Nature and Humanity, Studious Desire and Sensual Appetite, Experience and Ignorance—but the well-worn allegorical machinery is deftly turned to the service of the new learning. And as the only extant copy of the interlude is imperfect, probably less than half of Rastell's curriculum in dramatic form has been preserved.

If (as is probable) a third piece, *Calisto and Meliboea*, is rightly attributed to him, he brought on the stage not only representative types and personifications but individual figures. There were few more popular books throughout western Europe in the early sixteenth century than *Celestina*, a dramatic novel in twenty-one acts by the Spaniard Fernando de Rojaz. It tells of the passion of Calisto for the beautiful Meliboea, whose favour he wins through the wiles of the wanton Celestina; of the lovers' secret meetings, Calisto's accidental death, Meliboea's suicide, and the murder of Celestina. It was thus a story of the *Romeo and Juliet* type, and the English adapter who skilfully turned the first four acts into a play gave promise of providing our first romantic love-tragedy. But he breaks off abruptly after the meeting between Celestina and Meliboea to introduce the latter's father, who relates a warning dream, and then goes on to moralize about the training of the young, and the importance of good laws and law-givers. As Rastell shows elsewhere a special interest in dreams and as he always had an eye to social improvement, it seems likely that he was the author as well as the publisher of this incomplete adaptation. With his manifold interests, economic, scientific, and religious, he was, in his way, an early Tudor Bernard Shaw who put his dramatic gifts to propagandist use.

Now that we know more of what Medwall and Rastell did for English secular drama in its infancy, John Heywood has been deposed from the position that he long held as the first of our playwrights who was a known individual figure. It is no longer the custom to ascribe to him any anonymous play of his period, and there has even been a stricter inquisition into his right to some of those traditionally associated with his name. But when all these points have been considered he still takes the chief place in his group.

Recent research has thrown new light upon his personal career, about which mistaken statements have been current. He was born in 1497, and apparently entered the Court service in 1519. A first quarterly payment of £5 of a yearly salary of £20 was made to him at Michaelmas, 1519, and in a similar payment a year later, he is called a 'singer'. In February 1520/1 he was granted a further annuity of 10 marks (£6 13*s*. 6*d*.), and in the payment of the instalment of his salary and annuity at Michaelmas 1525 he is called 'player of the virginals'. In 1528 he was discharged from the King's Court, on a pension of £10 for life. Meanwhile through the Royal favour he had obtained City privileges. In May 1523, in response to a letter from the King, he was admitted to the Freedom of the City of London and he had probably by this time married John Rastell's daughter, Joan, and become a householder.

Though he had left, for the time, the Court service, he was in favour with Princess Mary, and in March 1537/8 he played an interlude with his 'children', probably boys of the song-school of St. Paul's Cathedral, before

John Heywood

From a woodcut in his allegorical Poem, *The Spider and the Flie* (printed 1556)

her. It is curious that in the following February he twice performed a mask of King Arthur's Knights before the head of the Protestant party, Thomas Cromwell, for he was an ardent Roman Catholic, and nearly lost his life in 1544 for taking part in a plot against Cranmer. Yet in March 1552 his pension was changed for one of £40 by Edward VI, before whom he took part in court entertainments. With the accession of Queen Mary in September 1553 his fortunes reached their highest pitch. On the day before her coronation the Queen rode from the Tower to Westminster. At the east end of St. Paul's, against the school, Heywood sat in a pageant under a vine and made an oration to her in English and Latin. Certain children and men (probably from Colet's foundation) sung 'diverse staves' in her honour. She stayed a good while and gave diligent ear to their song. In 1555 his pension was increased, and on 12 November 1558 he received a grant of lands. Five days later Mary died and the Elizabethan settlement put an end to Heywood's period of prosperity. He fled with his son, Ellis, in July 1564 to Flanders. In 1573 he was living at Malines, but in 1576 he was brought by Ellis to the Jesuit College at Antwerp. When this was attacked at Whitsuntide 1578 by a mob, the inmates, including the Heywoods, took refuge at Louvain. The date of the old man's death is uncertain, but in spite of exile and misfortune he kept his 'mad merry wit' to the last. When the priest at his death-bed kept repeating that the flesh was frail, Heywood bade his confessor beware of blaming God for not having made him a fish.

When Heywood died the golden age of Elizabethan letters was beginning with *Euphues* and *The Shepherd's Calendar*. But his dramatic work dates from half a century back, and in some respects it bears more distinctly the stamp of the old order than that of Medwall or Rastell. It does not have faint anticipations of Shakespeare or Shaw, but reproduces much of the spirit of Chaucer. Unfortunately when his 'Works' were printed in 1562, two years before his exile, they only included his collection of Proverbs and Epigrams. But in 1533 his brother-in-law William Rastell had printed *The Play of the Wether*, and in 1534 *A Play of Love*, each with Heywood's name on the title-page. And in the British Museum there is a manuscript play *Witty and Witless*, which concludes 'Amen q[uo]th John Heywood'.

These three plays of undisputed authorship form a group with allied features. They have no action but introduce various typical figures who present a subject from different angles. In *Witty and Witless* John and James dispute whether it is better to be a fool or a wise man. James makes out a clever case for the fool and gets the better of John, but Jerome appears on the scene and turns the tables in favour of the 'witty' or sensible man. *Love* is a somewhat similar debate on an abstract theme. 'The Lover not Loved' and 'The Woman Loved not Loving' contend as to who suffers the greater pain, while a parallel argument on pleasure takes place between 'The Lover Loved' and 'Neither Lover nor Loved'. The prolix argument ends in a draw in either case, but the speeches contain passages about emotional experiences which show Heywood's vivid narrative power.

There are internal indications that *Wether* like *Fulgens and Lucres*, was written for an entertainment in the hall of a great lord who provided supper for his guests. They must have had an enjoyable evening, for the interlude, written in the author's most genial vein, introduces a succession of representative characters with strong views on the most perennial of themes, the management of the weather. These characters are introduced in turn into the presence of Jupiter by his 'crier', Merry-Report, a voluble rogue. The gentleman wants dry and windless weather for hunting; the merchant asks for variable, but not violent, winds. The ranger of woods, the water-miller, and the wind-miller, each has his own petition. The gentlewoman dislikes sunshine, which spoils her complexion, while the 'launder' wants it to dry clothes for her. Lastly comes the Boy, 'the least', or smallest, 'that can play', crying to his godfather god:

> All my pleasure is in catching of birds,
> And making of snow-balls and throwing the same.

Hence he begs for

> great frost for my pitfalls
> And plenty of snow to make my snow-balls.

Jupiter finally announces that all the petitioners shall have in turn the weather they ask for, and Heywood seems to be a disciple of his father-in-law when he makes the god end by laying stress on the economic dependence of one class on another.

There is no reason to question Heywood's authorship of *The Four PP*, though it did not come from the Rastell press. It was published by W. Middleton, a printer of good repute, who ascribed it to him on the title-page. The suggestion has been made that its publication, probably about 1544, was a friendly act, at the time when Heywood was involved in the plot against Cranmer, to show that he was no obstinate reactionary. For of 'the four PP'—the palmer, the pardoner, the poticary, and the pedler—the two former are distinctive products of the old order and they are treated with stinging raillery. This pair of worthies and the poticary begin by disputing, after the Heywood fashion, about the merits of their respective callings. They ask the pedler who appears with a well-filled pack to decide between them. He protests that he cannot judge in matters of weight, but he offers to pronounce upon their relative merits in lying, if each will tell a tale to illustrate his powers in this respect. The poticary tells a pungent tale of a wonderful cure that he had effected. The pardoner caps this with an account of his visit to Hell to rescue the soul of his friend Margery Corson. The account of his interview with Lucifer on the anniversary day of his fall is a masterpiece of grotesque narrative, and as a sheer piece of humorous writing is far above anything that had yet appeared in any English play. Lucifer agrees to let Margery go on condition that no more women come to Hell, and his attendant devils roar with joy at getting rid of such a shrew.

At this point the palmer steps in. He cannot understand why women should be considered shrews in Hell, as in all his wanderings

> I never saw nor knew in my conscience
> Any one woman out of patience.

Such a declaration forces his rivals to give away their own case even before the adjudicator can find voice. The poticary cries, 'By the mass, there is a great lie', and the pardoner follows suit with 'I never heard a greater, by our lady', whereupon the pedler sums up with the question to which there is only one answer, 'A greater? nay, know ye any so great?' The palmer evidently takes the prize, but the pedler will not let the audience go without a final exhortation on faith and morals in the approved Heywood fashion.

There is no such edifying conclusion to the two 'merry plays', of *The Pardoner and the Frere* and *Johan Johan.* This is one reason for questioning their traditional ascription to Heywood, and it has also to be borne in mind that when William Rastell printed the plays in 1533 he did not assign them to his brother-in-law, though this may be due to the fact that they have no title-pages, merely a descriptive heading. On the other hand they form with *The Four PP* a unique trilogy at this period, written in a spirit of what has been called 'anti-clerical banter'. And some of the details introduced, as well as certain phrases, suggest that the three plays are from the same hand. The *Pardoner and the Frere* begins, much like *The Four PP*, with a recital by the two clerical worthies of the merits of their respective callings. They gradually pass to personal abuse and thence to fisticuffs. Hereupon the parson of the Church appears and gets to grips with the frere while he calls in his neighbour Prat to deal with the pardoner. At first they get the better in the struggle, but soon the pair of rascals turn the tables on them and go off triumphant.

In *Johan Johan* the satire is more acid. A henpecked husband, the Johan Johan of the title, has to fetch and carry, and chafe wax to mend a hole in a pail, while his wife Tyb is entertaining a priestly lover, Sir Jhan. But at last driven to desperation by their taunts he turns upon them and drives them out of his house.

Both of these plays, especially the second, have kinship with contemporary French farces, though the French 'amoureux' is not a cleric. The *Pardoner and the Frere* has also points of contact with an early poem of Sir Thomas More, *A mery Jest how a sergeant would learn to play the frere*. It has been suggested with good reason that Heywood may have written the trilogy when specially under the influence of More, and that it is even possible that the two anonymous plays were among the youthful comedies of Sir Thomas. These are important problems of 'higher criticism', as are also the exact dates of composition and the order of the plays that have been discussed in this chapter. But they do not affect the main conclusion of this survey that there is a well defined *corpus* of wellnigh a dozen early Tudor plays, written by men of various avocations, clerical, legal, and musical, but closely associated through ties of family or service. They had all a share of the culture of their day, and we can detect in their themes and the spirit of their plays here the influence of Chaucer, there of the new humanism, elsewhere of French farce. But their eye is mainly on the types and issues of their own changing age, and their dramatic technique is, for better or worse, essentially native. They are thus set apart from those who in the schools, the Inns of Court, and the Universities were soon to fit, as far as in them lay, English comedy and tragedy to the alien moulds of ancient Rome. To these playwrights we now turn.

II

COMEDY IN THE SCHOOLS—NICHOLAS UDALL

THE conditions of school life in Tudor times were in nearly all respects far harder than they became later. The hours were long; the curriculum narrow and rigid; holidays were few, games played a small part; the rod was in constant use. It is no wonder that the unfortunate boy, as known to Shakespeare, crept like a snail unwillingly to school.

But he had at least one compensation denied till quite recently to his successors. He could have the fun and excitement of acting in plays. The fact that boys performed the women's parts in the professional companies which were coming into being, and that the choir-boys of the Chapel Royal and St. Paul's Cathedral took part in entertainments and pageants, in which singing was a feature, helped to make it natural for the ordinary schoolboy to turn amateur actor. And though school-plays were instituted primarily with pedagogical aims, it was inevitable, as will be seen, for more than one reason, that they should become part of the general dramatic movement of the time.

The broad effect of the Renaissance on English education was liberalizing. The medieval school curriculum was chiefly restricted to the *trivium*, grammar, logic, and rhetoric, treated in a formal way. With the spread of the new learning from the Continent to Britain came the study of the masterpieces of Latin, and in a very minor degree of Greek, literature. They were valued, however, not so much for their contents as for their style, and as models of elegance of expression. And at a time when Latin was still the international language its oral use was no less important than its literary. Hence boys were set at first to learn phrases from dialogue books like the *Colloquies* of the great Dutch humanist, Erasmus, or the Spanish educational reformer, Vives. They passed on later to the oratory of Cicero and the conversational Latin of the two great Roman writers of comedy, Plautus and Terence. The latter, in especial, was regarded as a well of Latin undefiled. And to get the full benefit from these two masters of the ancient stage, it was soon found necessary not merely to read but to perform their plays. The words of a seventeenth-century schoolmaster, Charles Hoole of Rotherham, concerning Terence, might have been used by any of his early Tudor predecessors:

> When you meet with an act or scene that is full of affection and action, you may cause some of your scholars —after they have learned it—to act it first in private amongst themselves, and afterwards in the open school before their fellows. Herein you must have a main care of their pronunciation and acting every gesture to the very life.

But there was an important reason why such performances could not long be restricted to the 'open school' and an audience of schoolfellows. Latin, as has been said, was the international language, and when visitors of distinction came to England, a natural way of entertaining them was by the presentation of a play in that tongue. If *Fulgens and Lucres* was acted before the Spanish and Flemish ambassadors in 1497, in this case the vernacular was used; but for those who had 'a poor pennyworth of English' a Latin comedy was more appropriate. This was beyond the scope of professional players, and so a call was soon made by the highest in the land upon the services of the schoolmasters and their boy actors. St. Paul's grammar-school had been reorganized by Dean Colet in 1512, and made a centre of humanistic teaching. It is not known whether the St. Paul's boys performed the 'goodly comedy of Plautus' with which Henry VIII entertained some French hostages in 1520. But under their High Master, John Ritwise, they acted the *Phormio* of Terence in 1528 before Cardinal Wolsey. The boys of 'the grammar school of Westminster' appeared before Elizabeth in January 1564/5 in *Heautontimoroumenos* of Terence and *Miles Gloriosus* of Plautus.

But plays in Latin were not confined to those of the 'old masters'; they included neo-Latin works by continental and English humanists. Thus Ritwise is reported to have made 'the tragedy of Dido out of Virgil', to be acted by his boys before Wolsey. In 1565–6 when Princess Cecilia of Sweden was paying a rather troublesome visit to the English Court, Elizabeth and the Princess were present at a performance by the Westminster boys of an adaptation of *Sapientia Salomonis* by Sixt Birck of Basle. The copy of the play which, according to custom, was prepared for the Queen's use is still preserved among the British Museum MSS. (Add. 20061), with 'E.R.' both on the binding and on the illuminated title-page. A list of the expenses incurred is also extant, ranging from the payment to 'a woman that brought her childe to the stadge and there attended upon it' (evidently the subject of Solomon's judgement) to that for 'a haddocke occupied in the plaie'.

It was a natural step from Latin plays, new or old, to translations and English adaptations of them, and thence to original plays in the mother tongue. As early perhaps as 1520 a translation of *Andria* under the title *Terens in English*, was published by John Rastell—another of his varied services to the development of drama. And by the middle of the century the leading schools were busy acting plays classical, humanist, and vernacular of the most varied types. In some cases their statutes made this compulsory. When Westminster was re-founded by Elizabeth it was enacted under a penalty of ten shillings that between Christmas and Twelfthnight: 'ludimagister et preceptor simul Latine unam, magister choristarum Anglice alteram comoediam aut tragoediam a discipulis et choristis suis in aula privatim vel publice agendam curent.'

In addition to their performances of Latin plays already mentioned, there are payments on record for their Court performances of English plays, *Paris and Vienna*, 15 February 1572, and *Truth, Faithfulness, and Mercy*, 1 January 1574.

At Eton a document drawn up by the Head Master, William Malim, about 1560, before the visit of a Royal Commission throws interesting light upon the acting of the plays, and the reasons why it was encouraged. About the feast of St. Andrew (November 30) the 'ludimagister' was accustomed to choose

> scenicas fabulas optimas et quam accommodatissimas, quas pueri feriis natalitiis subsequentibus non sine ludorum elegantia, populo spectante, publice aliquando peragant. Histrionum levis ars est, ad actionem tamen oratorum et gestum motumque corporis decentem tantopere facit, ut nihil magis. Interdum etiam exhibet Anglico sermone contextas fabulas, quae habeant acumen et leporem.

It is evident from the mention in the last sentence of the occasional performance of plays in the English tongue that when speaking of 'scenicas fabulas optimas' he was referring to the Latin drama. We learn from Malim's statement that these Christmastide performances were public. Hence it is natural that the Eton boys at times took their plays up to great houses or the Court. In 1538 (as will be shown further) they acted before Cromwell; on 6 January 1573, they were seen by Elizabeth in a play at Hampton Court.

Under its first Head Master, Richard Mulcaster (1561–86), the newly-founded Merchant Taylors' School rivalled the older foundations in its dramatic activities. One of Mulcaster's pupils, later a well-known judge, has recorded that 'yeerly he presented sum players to the court, in which his scholars wear only actors, and I on among them, and by that meanes taughte them good behaviour and audacitye'. The dates of some of these performances, and the plays acted, are known to us from the records of payment. They include *Timoclea at the Siege of Thebes by Alexander* at Candlemas 1574, and *Ariodante and Genevora*, from an episode in Ariosto's *Orlando Furioso* on Shrove Tuesday, 1583. But curiously enough the Company themselves, from a sense of offended dignity, forbade after 16 March 1574 any performances in their own hall. On that date they passed the following resolution:

> Whereas at our common playes and such lyke exercises whiche be comonly exposed to be seene for money, everye lewd persone thinketh himself (for his peny) worthye of the chiefe and most comodious place withoute respecte of any other either for age or estimacion in the comon weale . . . as experience of late in this our comon hall hath sufficyently declared, where by reasone of the tumultuous disordered persones repayringe hither to see suche playes as by our schollers were here lately played, the Maisters of

this Worshipful Companie and their deare ffrends could not have entertaynmente and convenyente place as they ought to have had . . . yt is ordeyned and decreed . . . that henceforthe theire shall be no more plays suffered to be played in this our Comon Hall.

It was not only the schools in London or its neighbourhood that became active centres of amateur playing. It was fitting that the ecclesiastical capital, Canterbury, should take a lead in a movement of this kind, and the Dean and Chapter gave generous encouragement to the theatrical performances by the boys of the King's School. In the accounts of the Chapter from 1560 onwards payments are entered to the schoolmaster and scholars towards such expenses as they shall be at in setting forth of tragedies, comedies, and interludes at Christmas. In the north-west the boys of the town school at Shrewsbury gave performances in a quarry outside the walls; in the north-east Beverley, and in the home counties Hitchin, were noted for their school performances. From time to time additional records come to light showing how widespread was this form of 'community drama'. It is a field in which explorers of local archives may still hope to be of service to historians of the stage.

Among the schoolmaster playwrights the most representative figure is Nicholas Udall, though his theatrical activities had a wider range than the class-room. Born in Hampshire in 1505 he became a scholar of Winchester at the age of twelve, and of Corpus Christi College, Oxford, when he was fifteen. He took his B.A. in 1524, but his notoriety as an exponent of Lutheran views prevented him from proceeding M.A. till 1534. It was natural that with his protestant sympathies he should contribute verses to a pageant in honour of Anne Boleyn's coronation in May 1533. In February of the same year he published his *Floures for Latine spekynge selected and gathered oute of Terence*. The 'flowers' are phrases gathered from three plays of Terence with their English equivalents. He became in 1534 Head Master of Eton, where, if Thomas Tusser, one of his pupils, is to be trusted, he did not spare the rod. But he encouraged acting by his boys, and on 2 February 1537/8 was paid £5 for a performance by them before Thomas Cromwell. He left Eton under a cloud in 1541, having been charged with theft of part of the College plate, and having made a confession of immorality. If he was really guilty it is curious that he did not forfeit the regard of his friends or the favour of great personages. After publishing in 1542 a translation of the *Apophthegms* of Erasmus, he took part in a version of the same scholar's *Paraphrase* of the New Testament. The work was under the patronage of Catherine Parr, and Udall who himself undertook *St. Luke*, was able to get Princess Mary as a collaborator for part of *St. John*. He was thus occupied till the close of the reign of Henry VIII.

His religious views commended him to Edward and his Council, and he received more than one piece of ecclesiastical preferment. But even under Mary, perhaps on account of their previous literary association, he retained Court favour. In December 1554, a letter of the Queen states that he has at 'soondrie seasons' shown diligence in exhibiting 'Dialogues and Enterludes', and directs the Office of the Revels to provide him with such apparel as he may need for the Christmas entertainments. In accordance with this there is an entry in the Revels accounts for Christmas 1554 of charges for 'Maskes and plaies set owte by Vdall with alteracion of garmentes for his Actours from tyme to tyme as he did occupie them'.

Meanwhile he had returned to pedagogy and had become 'schoolmaster' to Gardiner, Bishop of Winchester, presumably in connexion with the chapel and household of the episcopal palace in Southwark. Gardiner died in November 1555, and a month later Udall was appointed Head Master of Westminster, a post that he held till his death on 23 December 1556.

The outline of Udall's varied activities during his comparatively short life is not only of interest in itself but has a close bearing on the canon of his plays which is even more difficult to determine than that of Heywood. We know that he was the author of *Ralph Roister Doister*, for Thomas Wilson, who was one of Udall's pupils at Eton, in the third edition of his *Arte of Logique*, January 1553/4, gives an example of 'ambiguitie', 'taken out of an interlude made by Nicholas Udall'. The example is a mispunctuated love-letter in Act III, Sc. iv, of *Roister Doister*. As the example is not given in the two earlier editions of the *Arte of Logique* (1551 and 1552), and as Wilson would naturally have there drawn upon an Eton play, it is probable that the comedy belongs to 1553 when Udall was schoolmaster to Gardiner. A recently discovered law-suit relating to 1551–3 in which he was defendant, throws light upon some of the allusions in the play.

Thus we can no longer connect *Roister Doister*, as used to be the fashion, with either Eton or Westminster. But the only surviving copy was presented in 1818 to the library of Eton. Its title-page is missing but it presumably belongs to the edition entered to Thomas Hacket in 1566. Uncertainty as to details does not,

College Hall, Westminster

From an engraving in R. Ackermann's *History of the Colleges of Winchester, Eton, and Westminster, &c.* (1816)

however, affect the importance of *Roister Doister* as the earliest extant English play showing the influence on technique and character-drawing of classical models. In that sense alone it can still be called the first of our comedies. For the looser texture of the interludes and dialogues of Medwall, Rastell, and Heywood, 'schoolmaster' Udall substituted an organic plot, arranged in Acts and Scenes after the fashion of Latin comedy. And he borrowed from Plautus some typical figures of the Roman stage, though he adapted them to English conditions. Roister Doister himself is a modern variant of the *Miles Gloriosus* or braggart soldier. He pays court to Dame Custance and her thousand pounds, though she is betrothed to Gawin Goodluck, who is absent on a sea-voyage. His chief confidant is Mathewe Merygreeke, who combines features of the classical parasite and *servus* with the tricksy humour of the Vice in the *Moralities*. It is Merygreeke who reads aloud Roister Doister's love-letter with a misplacing of the stops that reverses its meaning and thus infuriates Dame Custance. What a capital way of impressing on boys the importance of correct punctuation! It is Merygreeke too who urges the braggart, when the widow spurns his advances, to take revenge by making an attack upon her household. But with the aid of her merry, high-spirited maids armed with domestic weapons, she puts Roister Doister and his companions to shameful flight. She becomes for a moment a pathetic figure when Goodluck, upon a false report, suspects her of being untrue to him. But on his return he finds his mistake, and all ends happily with a reconciliation in which Roister Doister and Merygreeke are included.

The play with its fun and frolic, its songs, its classical types in a Tudor setting is very attractive. The recent revivals of it have proved that it is no less effective on the stage in the twentieth century than in the sixteenth. It is all the more tantalizing therefore that we cannot identify with certainty among extant plays any of the *comœdiæ plures* attributed by John Bale to Udall. But there are several to which, on one ground or another, he has a reasonable claim, or which at least may be assigned to his group.

Thus his name has recently been connected on plausible grounds with the authorship of *Thersites.* This is an adaptation of a neo-Latin dramatic dialogue by Ravisius Textor, in which the Homeric demagogue is burlesqued as a braggart who is first terrified by a snail, and afterwards, when challenged by a soldier, runs away dropping his sword and club. From a reference to the birth of Prince Edward (afterwards Edward VI) the piece seems to have been written in October 1537. In Udall's translation of the *Apophthegms* of Erasmus there is a note partly in prose, partly in verse, on Thersites,

> a pratleer, bee ye sure,
> Without all facion, ende or measure,

in much the same vein as the burlesque of him in the interlude. The piece, though more farcical than *Roister Doister*, shows something of the same skill in giving an English background to classical figures. If the adaptation was from Udall's pen, it was written or revived during his Eton period, though a reference to the proctor and his men and various local allusions strongly suggest that it was performed some time at an Oxford college.

Another play which resembles *Roister Doister* in technique though not in subject-matter is *The Historie of Jacob and Esau*, licensed for printing in 1557, and extant in an edition of 1568. It is a vivid dramatization of the Biblical story, with Esau as the chief figure. He has an insatiable passion for hunting which takes him abroad before daylight till late at night, so that Rebecca scarcely ever sees him and thus naturally favours Jacob. Esau's talkative servant, Ragau, Isaac's boy, Mido, Rebecca's handmaid, Abra, and Deborah the nurse, all inventions of the playwright, remind us of the household of Dame Custance, and the general reconciliation at the end breathes the same spirit as the close of *Roister Doister*. Both plays are divided into Acts and Scenes on the classical model, and have similar metrical characteristics. *Jacob and Esau* is thus either by Udall or by some dramatist of kindred type.

Respublica, preserved in a manuscript, was a 'Christmas devise' performed by boys in 1553. It has the formal division of Acts and Scenes and has been claimed for Udall. But it is unlikely that a Morality play of a politico-religious character written from a strongly Roman Catholic standpoint was from his pen. There is more to be said in favour of his authorship of the clever farce, *Jack Juggler* (entered in the Stationers' Register 1562, but written earlier). Here, as in *Roister Doister*, though on a much slighter scale, Plautus is laid under contribution. The underplot of his *Amphitruo*, in which Mercury impersonates a servant, is not only given an English dress, but is turned into a veiled attack on the doctrine of transubstantiation.

In any case, as has been recently suggested, it is probable that Udall's Lutheran sympathies found vent in a play which we know to be his but which has not survived. This is *Ezechias* (Hezekiah), acted before Queen Elizabeth on 8 August 1564 during a royal visit to Cambridge. It was played by members of King's College in the College Chapel, and as Udall was an Oxford man, this posthumous revival of one of his plays at Cambridge suggests that it was a composition of his Eton period familiar to some of those who had passed from the school to the allied society of King's. The revival was also probably intended to appeal to the Queen's religious prepossessions. From the accounts that remain of the performance, we know that it included among other episodes Hezekiah's destruction of the idols of the grove, and the mysterious annihilation of the Assyrian invaders by night. In the preface to his translation of the *Paraphrase* by Erasmus of St. Luke, which has been mentioned above, Udall had spoken of King Henry VIII as 'our Ezechias sent to roote up al Idolatry due to dead images of stone and tymber as unto God'. The reforming zeal of Hezekiah in the play probably therefore typified that of Elizabeth's father, and it is possible that Bale was referring to *Ezechias* when he included a *Tragoedia de papatu*, translated for Catherine Parr, among Udall's works. As a young man he had helped to celebrate in 1533 the coronation of the ill-fated Anne Boleyn, and now some thirty years later Anne's daughter heard his voice speaking to her, as it were, from the grave. Whatever difficulties there may be about determining the canon of his works, recent research has gone far to confirm his position as the most representative of English playwrights during those thirty years which lie between the main activities of Heywood's native dramatic production and the beginning of the strongly classicizing influences in the performances at the Inns of Court.

III

TRAGEDY AT THE INNS OF COURT

THE school play, though it became diverted to lighter purposes, had an educational origin and a didactic aim. It was otherwise with the performances which from the early years of Elizabeth's reign the lawyers arranged in their metropolitan academes, the Inns of Court. These adult lovers of dramatic art were aiming at the entertainment of themselves and their guests, including, on occasion, the sovereign herself. They might take the opportunity of moralizing, as befitted their professional status, upon problems of government. But the plays and revels at the Middle and Inner Temples and at Gray's Inn were intended frankly for recreation. We have an interesting memorial, dating from the later years of the Queen's reign, of the spirit in which these entertainments were organized and of the pains lavished upon them. *Gesta Grayorum* is an account of the revels at Gray's Inn, 1594–5, when Mr. Henry Helmes, a Norfolk gentleman, was elected to be a mock king, with the title of Prince of Purpoole, and an array of officers, and was enthroned in the great hall on 20 December, St. Thomas's eve. On Innocents' Day (28 December) he received an ambassador from the Inner Temple 'attended by a great number of brave Gentlemen'. But there was such a crowd on the stage that no entertainment could be presented till late in the evening when 'a Comedy of Errors was played by the players', probably Shakespeare's comedy performed by the Lord Chamberlain's men. There was better fortune with a show on Twelfth Night, and at Shrovetide the Prince of Purpoole visited the Queen at Court and presented a *Masque of Proteus*, which won Elizabeth's commendation of the actors, 'and in general of Gray's Inn as a House that she was much beholden unto, for that it did always study for some sports to present unto her'. The compliment was well deserved, for Gray's Inn and the Inner Temple had for over thirty years vied with each other in entertaining the Queen. But their 'sports' had for the most part taken a more austere form than the mask, and it is among the historic glories of the English Bar that its members were the first to produce a blank-verse tragedy upon a London stage. The presentation of *Gorboduc or Ferrex and Porrex* at the Christmas revels of the Inner Temple, 1561–2, and its repetition before Elizabeth at Whitehall on 18 January 1562, marked a new departure of the highest importance for the future of English drama.

When seventy years later Milton in *Il Penseroso* made his invocation:

> Sometime let gorgeous Tragedy
> In sceptred pall come sweeping by,
> Presenting Thebes, or Pelops' line,
> Or the tale of Troy divine,

he, who had been turning over Greek as well as Latin writers, was thinking specially of the glories of the Attic stage. But to the lawyers of the Inns of Court, and to the bulk of the Elizabethan intelligentsia, classical tragedy was chiefly represented by the plays of Seneca, the philosopher and dramatist of the age of Nero. In them melodrama had taken the place of the austere pain of truly tragic art, and sententious moralizing had displaced the dialogue that reveals character in action. But they had a sombre power, and they made effective use of much of the traditional machinery of Greek tragedy—the Messenger, the

Queen Elizabeth
From the painting in the National Portrait Gallery

Nurse, and the Ghost. Over the men of the Renaissance age these Latin plays exercised a veritable fascination. They were translated and they were imitated, both in Latin and in the vernacular tongues, in Italy and in France. England was now to follow suit. In the three years previous to the production of *Gorboduc*, three of Seneca's plays, *Troas*, *Thyestes*, and *Hercules Furens*, had been successively published in English versions by Jasper Heywood, a Fellow of All Souls College, Oxford. Jasper was the son of John Heywood, and it is an irony of our dramatic history that Seneca should have been first sponsored by a direct descendant of the leading playwright of the native school. It can scarcely be a mere coincidence that the appearance of these plays in English dress should have been immediately followed, in 1562, by the writing and performance of the first Elizabethan tragedy on the Senecan model.

But though it borrows the machinery of the Roman stage, *Gorboduc* is far from being a pale replica of a Latin forerunner. Its authors, Thomas Norton and Thomas Sackville, were active men of affairs, and members of Elizabeth's first Parliament. Sackville (afterwards Lord Buckhurst and Earl of Dorset) was to divert to the service of the State those high gifts which in the *Induction* to the *Mirror for Magistrates* had given promise of a poetic achievement that might have placed him beside Sidney and Spenser. Thomas Norton took a prominent part in the Parliamentary debates on the question of the succession to the throne. Thus when they combined in dramatic composition for the entertainment of their Inn (Norton according to the first unauthorized edition of 1565 being responsible for Acts I–III and Sackville for IV–V), they chose a subject from early British 'history', which was not then as now harshly differentiated from legend, and which lent itself to topical application. The 'argument' or plot of the tragedy is thus set forth:

> *Gorboduc* king of Brittaine, diuided his realme in his life time to his sonnes, *Ferrex* and *Porrex*. The sonnes fell to dyuision and discention. The yonger killed the elder. The mother that more dearely loued the elder, for reuenge killed the yonger. The people moued with the crueltie of the fact, rose in rebellion and slew both father and mother. The nobilitie assembled and most terribly destroyed the rebels. And afterwardes for want of issue of the prince whereby the succession of the crowne became vncertaine they fell to ciuill warre, in which both they and many of their issues were slaine, and the land for a long time almost desolate and miserably wasted.

The 'argument' is thus compact of violence, of murder, and warfare, but not a drop of blood is shed upon the stage. With an exaggeration of classical scruples the dramatists report all these atrocities through the lips of messengers. No action takes place before the eyes of the audience, and the dialogue in the first four Acts consists mainly of consultations between the various royalties and their advisers. In the last Act the question of the vacant succession is debated less with an eye to the Britain of Gorboduc than to the England of Elizabeth. And the sage statesman Eubulus is really urging the childless Tudor Queen to settle the succession during her lifetime and not leave it to be determined after her death (v. ii):

> Alas, in Parliament what hope can be
> When is of Parliament no hope at all?
>
> . . . .
>
> No, no: then Parliament should haue been holden,
> And certeine heires appointed to the crowne,

To stay the title of established right,
And in the people plant obedience,
While yet the prince did liue, whose name and power
By lawfull sommons and authoritie
Might make a Parliament to be of force,
And might haue set the state in quiet stay.

The sententiousness of the dialogue lessens the importance of the moralizing Choruses which on the Senecan model were appended to the first four Acts. Of a quite different origin, either from the spectacular *intermedii* or *entremets* popular in Italian plays, or from the allegorical tableaux associated with city pageants and court masks, were the dumb shows which precede each Act. Each dumb show began with the music of appropriate instruments and had its special signification. An example is that before Act IV:

> First the musick of Howboies began to plaie during which there came from vnder the stage, as though out of hell, three furies, Aletco, Megera, and Ctesiphone, clad in black garmentes sprinkled with bloud and flames, their bodies girt with snakes, their heds spred with serpentes in stead of heare, the one bearing in her hand a Snake, the other a Whip, and the third a burning Firebrand: ech driuing before them a king and a queene, which moued by furies vnnaturally had slaine their owne children . . . after that the furies and these had passed about the stage thrise, they departed and than the musicke ceased: hereby was signified the vnnaturall murders to follow, that is to say. Porrex slaine by his owne mother. And of King Gorboduc and queen Viden, killed by their owne subiectes.

Thus *Gorboduc* mingled modern with ancient machinery, and (as Sir Philip Sidney was afterwards to lament) did not observe those Unities of Time and Place which the Renaissance age mistakenly thought to be essentials of classical tragedy. But the two lawyer-playwrights borrowed from Senecan drama the structural division into Acts. And above all it was in imitation of Seneca's unrhymed metre that (disregarding the difference between quantity and stress as bases of prosody) they introduced blank verse to the English stage. Some lines from the concluding speech of Eubulus have been quoted above, but in another vein is the lament by the court lady Marcella for the murdered Prince Porrex (IV. ii):

> Ah noble prince, how oft haue I behelde
> Thee mounted on thy fierce and traumpling stede,
> Shining in armour bright before the tilt,
> And with thy mistresse sleue tied on thy helme,
> And charge thy staffe to please thy ladies eye,
> That bowed the head peece of thy friendly foe?
> How oft in armes on horse to bend the mace?
> How oft in armes on foote to breake the sworde,
> Which neuer now these eyes may see againe.

The lines, though unrhymed, have still something of the stanzaic movement which was natural to the author of the *Induction*, but they are not unworthy to be heralds, from afar off, of the blank-verse melodies of Marlowe, Shakespeare, and Fletcher.

It may well have been that the first publication of *Gorboduc* in 1565 stimulated the members of Gray's Inn to emulate their brethren of the Inner Temple by the production in 1566 of another tragedy in classical form. *Jocasta* as presented in the hall of the Inn was the joint work of George Gascoigne (who was to prove himself one of the most versatile of the Elizabethans) and of Francis Kinwelmersh. But unlike Sackville and Norton they were merely translators of an Italian original by the Venetian Lodovico Dolce whose *Giocasta* was itself a free version of a Latin rendering of the *Phoenissae* of Euripides. Thus *Jocasta* has nothing of the interest which attaches to *Gorboduc* as a neo-Senecan treatment of a theme professedly from national history, and turned into 'a tract for the times'. But it was a memorable event when authentic Greek tragedy even in this pale reflex, stepped upon London boards, and when consecrated figures of the Attic stage in its meridian splendour, Creon and Oedipus, Jocasta and Antigone, Polynices and Eteocles, spoke for the first time in English blank verse. For *Jocasta* followed *Gorboduc* in the use of this new poetic form and also in the introduction of dumb shows and 'musics' before every Act. From the detailed description of these and from the stage-directions it is evident that Gray's Inn spared nothing to secure spectacular effects. Whether both sexes were present or not at the performance, Gascoigne evidently expected them to be readers of the play. For he explained in the 1575 edition of his *Posies*, where it is included, that 'certain words which are not common in vse are noted and expounded in the margent . . . at request of a gentlewoman who vnderstode not poetycall words or termes'.

A more direct appeal to feminine interest was made by the Inner Temple play of 1567–8, *Gismond of Salerne*, acted before the Queen and her 'maids' to whom three prefatory sonnets are addressed. Each of the five Acts had a different author, but they all wrote in alternately rhyming quatrains. When, however, Robert Wilmot, who was responsible for the last Act, revised the play for publication in 1591, he substituted blank verse for the rhymed quatrains, as more befitting 'the decorum of these daies', and he gave the play the title of *Tancred and Gismunda* from the two chief characters. It is noticeable that in our three earliest extant serious plays dealing with love, the relation of the heroine and her father is emphasized. Medwall's Lucres is the 'chief jewel and riches' of Fulgens; Rastell cuts short the love-story of Meliboea to bring her moralizing father upon the stage; and in the Inner Temple tragedy Tancred, King of Naples and Prince of Salerne, is the agent of his ill-starred daughter's fate.

The plot is borrowed from the *Decameron*, but the quintet of lawyers who adapted it to their stage were not satisfied to allow Boccaccio's moving story to work its effect through pity and fear. Gismond driven by her father's despotic selfishness into a secret intrigue; Tancred's discovery of this; his barbarous vengeance upon the young lover, whose heart he sends in a golden cup to his daughter; her suicide followed by that of the remorse-stricken Tancred—what more could the Tragic Muse ask for her purposes? But the gentlemen of the Inner Temple borrowed materials from Seneca and Dolce; they brought Cupid down from Heaven and Megaera up from Hell; they introduced dumb-shows. Above all in their treatment of Gismond herself, and through the lips of the Chorus, '4 gentlemen of Salern', they made of her not a tragic heroine, but an example of ill-regulated passion whose fate has a warning, though (according to the Epilogue) one not needed by English womanhood:

Sufficeth to mainteine
The vertues which we honor in yow all:
So as our Britain ghostes, when life is past,
May praise in heuen, not plaine in Plutoes hall
Our dames, but hold them vertuous and chast,

Worthy to liue where furie neuer came,
Where Loue can see, and beares no deadly bowe;
Whoes lyues eternall tromp of glorious fame
With ioyfull sound to honest eares shall blow.

So long as the lawyers were thus bent on edification the legendary history of Britain afforded them apter material than the love-stories of Italy. When the gentlemen of Gray's Inn performed before the Queen on 28 February 1588, at her Court in Greenwich, *The Misfortunes of Arthur* 'reduced into tragicall notes by Thomas Hughes', one wonders whether Elizabeth remembered the warnings in *Gorboduc* a quarter of a century before on the dangers of civil faction, and their realization in the Throgmorton and Babington conspiracies and the other seditious movements that had brought Mary Stuart to the block at Fotheringay in the previous February, a year ago. Had Hughes that event, and Elizabeth's hesitation before signing the death-warrant, in mind when he makes the Chorus declare:

The wickeds death is safety to the iust.
To spare the Traitors, was to spoile the true,
Of force he hurtes the good that helpes the bad?

But *The Misfortunes of Arthur*, though it shows civil war in Britain, with the foreign aid of 'Saxons, Irish, Normans, Pictes and Scottes' on the one side, and of 'Islandians, Gothes, Noruegians, Albanes, Danes' on the other, is less politically 'tendencious' than *Gorboduc*. It is more directly Senecan in inspiration. From Geoffrey of Monmouth and from Malory the Gray's Inn playwright pieced together a plot of passion, crime, and incest as lurid as any known to the stage of imperial Rome. Uther Pendragon in guilty intercourse with Igerna, wife of Gorlois, Duke of Cornwall, whom he slays in warfare, begets twin children, Arthur and Anne. Of their incestuous union is afterwards born Mordred, who, while Arthur is waging war in France, gains the love of the Queen, Guenevora, and usurps his father's crown. All this is told in the Argument and more allusively by the Ghost of Gorlois, who like the Ghost of Tantalus in the *Thyestes*, opens the play with imprecations upon Mordred, Guenevora, and Arthur now returning in triumph from overseas. The play itself shows the working out of the doom thus denounced upon Pendragon's brood, and the death of Arthur and Mordred by each others' hands in battle in Cornwall, the scene of Uther's unlawful love.

So closely does Hughes follow the style of Seneca that many of the speeches in *The Misfortunes of Arthur* are for the most part translations of lines from the Roman dramatist's plays. This, it has been suggested, would appeal to the Queen who had herself tried her hand at an English version of a chorus in the *Hercules Oetaeus*, a play ascribed to Seneca. And in addition to the Ghost full use is made of the familiar Senecan machinery, especially of the Nuntius or Messenger, whose description in Act IV. ii of the battle, fatal to both father and son, shows the vigour with which the Gray's Inn dramatist could at his best handle blank verse:

> There *Mordred* fell, but like a Prince he fell,
> And as a braunch of greate *Pendragons* grafte
> His life breaths out, his eyes forsake the Sunne,
> And fatall Cloudes inferre a lasting Clips.[1]
> There *Arthur* staggering scant sustaind him selfe,
> There *Cador* founde a deepe and deadly wound,
> There ceast the warres, and there was *Brytaine* lost.

[1] Eclipse.

In the characterization of Arthur, however, Hughes shakes off the Senecan trammels and gives us something of an original figure, the old and war-weary king forced against his own will to do battle against his own son and on his native soil:

What couer (ah) for all my warres shall shrowde
My bloodlesse age; what seate for due deserts?
What towne, or field for auncient Souldiers rest?
What house? What roofe? What walls for weried lims?

Here Arthur becomes a figure of true pathos; no mere automatic victim of avenging doom.

There seem always to have been more hands than one in these Inns of Court tragedies. Though the play was by Hughes, for some reason instead of the opening and closing speeches penned by him for the Ghost of Gorlois two others by William Fulbecke were substituted. Two choruses were added by Francis Flower, and among those who devised the dumb shows which, after the fashion of *Gorboduc*, preceded each Act, was Francis Bacon who was thus gaining some practical experience of stage production. Was he allowed by his collaborators to put in practice the maxim set forth later in his essay on 'Masques and Triumphs' that 'since Princes will have such things it is better they should be graced with elegancy than daubed with cost?'

By 1588 the day had come when Tragedy was no longer to be the nursling of the lawyers in their Inns and was to attain its full estate on the public stage. But it owes a permanent debt to its scholarly foster-parents, who attuned its lisping accents to the use of blank verse. And almost equally notable was their service to English Comedy which at a Gray's Inn performance first spoke in prose. Medwall, Rastell, Heywood, and Udall had all used rhyming metres. When George Gascoigne produced his *Supposes* at Gray's Inn in 1566 (the same year as *Jocasta*) he might well have followed in their steps, for the play was a version of Ariosto's *Gli Suppositi*, a comedy of intrigue, and the Italian dramatist after writing it in prose had rewritten it in verse. Gascoigne seems to have used both the Italian forms, but his own version is in lively and fluent prose. Thus *Supposes*, though a translation, is a landmark in the history of English comedy. It was the flexible and scintillating instrument of prose here first used that was to give full scope to the humorous genius of Shakespeare, of Congreve, of Sheridan, and of Bernard Shaw.

And though it does not belong to the Inns of Court series, mention may here be made of another prose play of George Gascoigne, *The Glasse of Government* (1575), which is one of the most notable English examples of a dramatic type that had a widespread continental vogue. In the Low Countries especially a group of schoolmaster playwrights had written a series of Latin dramas on the Biblical subject of the Prodigal Son. Their aim was to introduce their students to elegant Latinity, without the moral contamination of Roman comedy, and to draw moral lessons from the story of the Prodigal. The most famous play in this cycle, *Acolastus*, by a schoolmaster in The Hague, was turned into English by John Palsgrave in 1540. The *Disobedient Child* by Thomas Ingelend (printed about 1560) was a free adaptation of another continental piece. Far more original was the striking anonymous play *Misogonus*, preserved in a partly mutilated manuscript, which is influenced by foreign Prodigal Son plays, but which introduces a number of powerfully drawn characters from the dramatist's own observation of English country life.

There is nothing of this masterly realism in *The Glasse of Government*, which returns to the more orthodox model of the continental Prodigal Son play, and which lays its scene in Antwerp. Its merit lies less in characterization than in construction. It introduces two fathers, each with a virtuous and a good-for-nothing son. The behaviour of the two exemplary youths, and of the scapegraces is contrasted at school, at the University, and in after life, and the lesson that evil courses bring condign punishment in the end is strongly enforced. Gascoigne shows himself more relentless than his Dutch models who had allowed Acolastus and Asotus, after the manner of the younger son in the parable, to repent and be forgiven. His departure from the spirit of the original story in St. Luke's Gospel was a sign that the day of the Prodigal Son dramatic cycle was passing. But had Shakespeare its popularity in mind when he made so many allusions to the story, and relied on his audience at once grasping the meaning of Launce's distortion in *The Two Gentlemen of Verona*, 'I have received my proportion, like the prodigious son'?

IV

STAGE-PLAYS AT OXFORD AND CAMBRIDGE

LONDON had the monopoly of Inns of Court plays, and was the chief, though by no means the only, centre of school performances. The third branch of Elizabethan academic drama had its home not in the Capital, but in the two Universities. In the annals of the English medieval stage Oxford and Cambridge play a surprisingly small part. No extant *Miracle* or *Morality* play is associated with them, though the account books of Magdalen College, Oxford, include expenses for what appear to be liturgical plays in the Chapel, and a drama on St. Mary Magdalene in 1506–7, probably acted in the Hall. There are earlier entries in the King's College, Cambridge, account-books from 1482 onwards of payments for Christmas plays, but there is nothing to indicate whether they were religious or otherwise.

There is more trace of the mummeries so dear to the Middle Ages, in which a mock dignitary, ecclesiastical or secular, was invested with temporary authority and the insignia and pomp of office. The most remarkable of these was the Boy-Bishop, the choir-boy who on the feast of the Holy Innocents or on St. Nicholas Day, exercised episcopal functions. Provision was made for him in the statutes of New College, Oxford, and King's College, Cambridge, and there is other evidence of him at All Souls and Magdalen, Oxford.

We hear at New College and Magdalen also of 'the Christmas Lord', who held sway over the merry-making at the Nativity season. He was in office also, in the middle of the sixteenth century in the more recent foundations of Christ Church and St. John's, and the latter College still preserves, though it falls just outside of the Tudor period, the detailed manuscript account of the reign of its Christmas Lord or Prince in 1607–8 with the plays acted in his honour. At St. John's College, Cambridge, Henry VIII enacted that each of the Fellows should be Christmas Lord in turn, under heavy penalties for failure. There were 'Lords' or 'Kings' at Christ's College and King's, while at Trinity, Cambridge, the still loftier title of 'Imperator' or Emperor was used, on the suggestion, as he tells us, of the astrologer, John Dee.

But most distinctive of all was the name given to the 'Lord' at Merton College, Oxford, *Rex Fabarum* or 'King of Beans'. The election to this office is recorded in 1485, the year in which the manuscript *Register* of the College begins, and this is said to be in accordance with ancient custom. From that date the list of the 'Kings' is given annually till 1539, and according to Anthony Wood, the historian of the University, who himself belonged to Merton, the last holder of 'that commendable office' was Jasper Heywood, son of John Heywood, in 1557. Wood has given an interesting account, based on college tradition in the seventeenth century of how the 'King of Beans' was elected.

> On the 19th of November, being the vigil of S. Edmund, King and Martyr, letters under seal were pretended to have been brought from some place beyond sea, for the election of a King of Christmas, or Misrule, sometimes called with us of the aforesaid College, Rex Fabarum. The said letters being put into the hands of the Bachelour Fellows, they brought them into the Hall that night, and standing, sometimes walking, round the fire, there reading the contents of them, would choose the senior

> Fellow that had not yet borne that office . . . and being so elected had power put into his hands of punishing all misdemeanours done in the time of Christmas either by imposing exercises on the juniors, or putting into the stocks at the end of the Hall any of the servants, with other punishments that were sometimes very ridiculous. He had always a chair provided for him, and would sit in great state when any speeches were spoken, or justice to be executed, and so this his authority would continue till Candlemas.

Thus traces of typical medieval buffoonery and topsy-turvydom lingered on in Renaissance Oxford and Cambridge. But with the rise of the 'new learning' in the Universities there came a development of drama within their confines due to the same general causes as operated in the schools with kindred results. But the scholars on the Isis and the Cam, though younger than their successors to-day, were a stage more advanced than the pupils of Udall and Mulcaster; they were in residence almost the whole of the year, including the seasons like Christmas specially associated with merry-making and pageantry; they could make use for their 'shows' of the halls of such magnificent sixteenth-century foundations as Christ Church and Trinity, and in many cases the regular performance of plays was enjoined upon them by the College statutes. It was the College system with its closely-knit corporate life that gave so powerful a stimulus to dramatic production at Oxford and Cambridge.

The pious founders had for the most part, if not exclusively, Greek and Latin plays in mind. And in the first half of the sixteenth century the English scholars seem usually to have staged comedies or tragedies by classical dramatists or their continental humanist imitators. But they soon began to strike out on their own account, though at first using the classical tongues. John Christopherson, who became Master of Trinity College, Cambridge, in the first year of Queen Mary's reign, wrote a tragedy in Greek on the subject of Jephthah and his daughter which is still preserved in the College library, though we do not know whether it was acted. The earliest extant Latin academic plays written by an Englishman, though printed at Cologne, are the *Christus Redivivus* (pr. 1543) and the *Archipropheta* (pr. 1548) of Nicholas Grimald, who is well known as a writer of verse through his contributions to *Tottel's Miscellany*. Grimald, who had been for three years a member of Christ's College, Cambridge, migrated to Oxford in 1540, and first became a member of Brasenose College, where his *Christus Redivivus*, a play on the Resurrection, was performed. In 1547 he was elected to Christ Church, for which he wrote his more notable play, *Archipropheta*, on the subject of John the Baptist. But though John is the titular figure, it is the amorous passion of Herod and Herodias that is in the forefront, and that gives the play a semi-romantic atmosphere.

We have seen how much the performances at the Inns of Court owed to the presence and the patronage of Elizabeth. So too drama at the Universities got a welcome stimulus from two memorable royal visits in 1564 and 1566. On 5 August 1564 the Queen arrived in Cambridge and took up her residence in the Lodge of the Provost of King's College. There was an elaborate programme in honour of her visit, including a series of theatrical performances. It had been proposed that these should take place in King's College Hall, and a stage had been erected there. But it had been found not to be large enough and to be inconveniently far from the Lodge. So at her own cost the Queen had another stage put up in the College chapel, and here on Sunday evening, 6 August, the *Aulularia* was acted. There can seldom have been a scene more typical of the pagan aspect of the Renaissance than this Sunday performance in a sacred building before Elizabeth of a comedy by Plautus. It lasted from nine o'clock till twelve, and the Queen enjoyed it more than some of her suite who had not 'a penny worth in' Latin.

On Monday evening another Latin play on the subject of Dido, written by Edward Halliwell, formerly a Fellow of King's, was acted, and this was followed on Tuesday by Udall's English tragedy, *Ezechias*, to which reference has been already made.[1] Three successive nights of play-going at the end of fully occupied days were too much even for Elizabeth, and she was not able to attend what had been planned as the final performance, on Wednesday, of a Latin version of the *Ajax* of Sophocles. It had to be abandoned, to the keen disappointment of the University, especially as great 'preparations and charges' had been employed upon it.

Two years later, on 31 August 1566, the Queen began a similar though slightly longer visit to Oxford. She stayed in Christ Church, and here too she had a stage put up at her own cost, though in the Hall, not the Cathedral. As at Cambridge the performances began on a Sunday night, 1 September, but the Queen who had had an exhausting day was not present and thus missed *Marcus Geminus*, a Latin comedy in prose, a curious new experiment by several Christ Church scholars. She appeared, however, on the following evening, in spite of a calamitous episode. There had

[1] See above, pp. 27-8.

been a widespread report of the magnificence of the scenic arrangements, and the pressure of the crowd on the steps at the entrance to the Hall, after the Queen and Court had passed in, was so great that a wall gave way, killing three persons and injuring others.

The play with this ominous prelude was Part I of *Palamon and Arcyte* by Richard Edwardes. Part II, after a night's interval, was given on 4 September. Edwardes had been a student of Christ Church in 1547, and in 1561 (as will be seen more fully below) he had been appointed Master of the Children of the Chapel Royal. He was thus uniquely fitted to superintend the theatrical arrangements for the Queen's entertainment at Oxford, besides contributing his own two-part play. Its loss is even more regrettable than that of Udall's *Ezechias*. But a detailed account by a contemporary spectator gives us a clear idea of the plot which followed closely the lines of Chaucer's *Knight's Tale*. Part I dealt with the rivalry of the two kinsmen Palamon and Arcite for the lady Emily, and with their fight in a wood where they are discovered by Duke Theseus and his hunting party. Part II contained the tournament decreed by the Duke between the two wooers, the victory of Arcite, his sudden death, and the betrothal of Palamon and Emily.

It would appear from an incident related by an eyewitness that use must have been made of the great Quadrangle in Christ Church in the staging of the hunting-scene:

> At ye crie of ye houndes in ye Quadrant uppon ye trayne of a foxe in ye huntinge of Theseus, when ye boyes in ye wyndowes cried 'nowe, nowe', 'o excellent', saide ye Queene, 'those boyes are readie to leape out at windowes to followe ye houndes'.

Other exclamations of Elizabeth, showing her interest and appreciation, are recorded. She said of Arcite that he was 'a right Martiall Knight havinge a swart countenance and a manly face'; and when a stander-by tried to stay the arm of the actor who was throwing a rich cloak upon his funeral pyre, she cried out 'goo, foole, he knoweth his part'. At the end she ordered that the young actor who had played Emily should have a reward 'for gatheringe her flowers prettily in ye garden and singinge sweetlie in ye pryme of March'. On the following evening, 5 September, a Latin tragedy on the subject of Progne's revenge on her husband King Tereus closed the series of entertainments, and next day the Queen rode away 'with many thanks to the whole University and repeated, fond farewells to her dear scholars'.

The two royal visits not only created a new standard of sumptuousness in academic theatrical productions, but they emphasized their value for entertainment as well as for educational ends. Thus mingled with classical and neo-Latin plays were the vernacular attractions of *Ezechias* and *Palamon and Arcyte*. And the same diversity is to be seen during the years that followed. An English comedy, *Gammer Gurtons Nedle*, which had been acted at Christ's College, Cambridge, was published in 1575, but there are grounds for supposing that it had been in print since 1563 and that its performance had preceded the Queen's visit. Indeed, a reference in Act V to 'arrest in the King's name' has suggested that it may date from the reign of Edward VI or even of Henry VIII. It would be easier to settle this point if we knew who the author was. The title-page speaks of him merely as 'Mr. S. M^{r} of Art'. This Mr. S. was

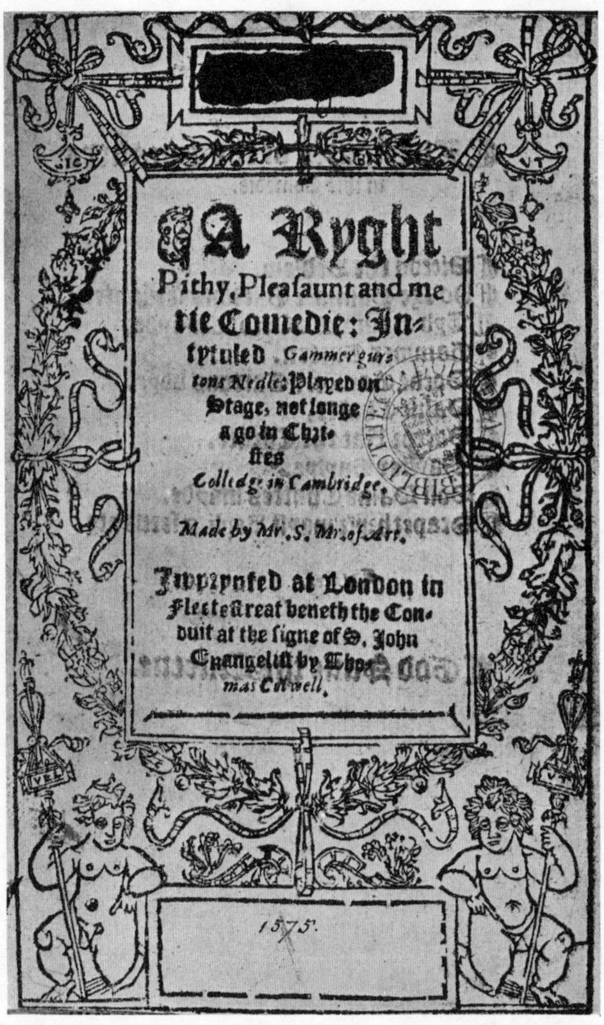

A Ryght
Pithy, Pleasaunt and me
rie Comedie: In-
tytuled Gammer gur-
tons Nedle: Played on
Stage, not longe
a go in Chri-
stes
Colledge in Cambridge.

Made by Mr. S. Mr. of Art.

Imprynted at London in
Fleetestreat beneth the Conduit at the signe of S. John
Evangelist by Tho-
mas Colwell.

1575.

Title-page of *Gammer Gurtons Nedle*
Printed by Thomas Colwell, 1575
From the copy in the Bodleian Library

certainly not John Still, an M.A. of Christ's College, afterwards Bishop of Bath and Wells, to whom the play has been mistakenly assigned; he may have been William Stevenson, M.A. in 1553, and a Fellow of the College, who took a lead in its dramatic activities. But a pamphleteer of 1588, who must have seen the 'Mr. S.' edition nevertheless definitely assigns it to John Bridges of Pembroke Hall, Cambridge, M.A. in 1560, and afterwards Dean of Salisbury and Bishop of Oxford. If he is right, 'Mr. S.' was a mistake or a blind by the publisher, and the play, though acted at Christ's, was by a man from another college. It is an odd tangle, but whoever the author may have been he united gifts of plot-construction, probably sharpened by study of classical models, to an eye for the humours and idiosyncrasies of English rural life. The plot turns upon the loss of Gammer Gurton's dearly cherished 'neele', or needle, and the complications that ensue in the village-community. These are largely due to the mischievous humour of Diccon the Bedlam, a vagabond beggar and rogue who is the central figure of the play. But it is he also who unwittingly leads to the discovery of the lost treasure when he smites Hodge the Gammer's farm-servant upon his breeches. Hodge, with a shriek of pain, discovers that the needle has all the time been sticking in his hinder-garment.

Hodge. Chave it by the masse, Gammer!
Gam. What? not my neele, Hodge?
Hodge. Your neele, Gammer! your neele . . .
Gam. 'Tis my own deare neele, Hodge, sykerly I wot!
Hodge. Cham I not a good sonne, Gammer, cham I not?

These few lines illustrate the metre of the play, the rhyming 'fourteener', and also the use in it of the south-western dialect (where 'chave' = 'I have' and 'cham'

= 'I am'), which became the convention for rustic speech in Elizabethan literature.

Another Cambridge play whose authorship has been in dispute is the Latin comedy, *Pedantius*, not published till 1631, but dating probably from half a century earlier. Thomas Nashe ascribed it to a Fellow of Trinity, Anthony Wingfield, but it has been shown to be from the pen of one of his colleagues, Edward Forsett. Nashe is, however, right in identifying the 'pedant' of the title with the Cambridge scholar Gabriel Harvey, whom he describes as full drawn in this 'exquisite comedy' and 'delineated from the sole of the foot to the crown of his head'. These words are unjust, for Harvey, the friend of Spenser, had real learning and literary gifts. But he was pompous and vain, and anxious to cut a figure in society. We can imagine how his enemies in the University shook their sides when they saw him pitilessly caricatured, making unsuccessful love to a slave-girl (taken over from classical comedy) and dunned by his tailor, to both of whom he spouts high-flown phrases taken in part from his own writings.

Of nearly the same date as *Pedantius* is one of the most notable of Cambridge neo-Senecan plays, *Richardus Tertius*, by Thomas Legge, Master of Caius College, which was acted at St. John's in the spring of 1580. It was planned on an elaborate scale, including the main events in the career of Richard of Gloucester from the death of Edward IV to the battle of Bosworth Field. It was divided into three Parts or *Actiones*, performed on successive evenings; it paid no regard to the Unities, and it dispensed with the Chorus. But it portrayed Richard in the conventional colours of a Senecan tyrant, and its language and metre were in the orthodox pattern of Roman tragedy. Shakespeare may have known something of the play. At any rate some of the features of his *Richard III*, especially the wooing of Anne in Act I, are anticipated by Legge and not by any of the chroniclers. A characteristic story is told by Fuller about John Palmer, a Fellow of St. John's, who acted Richard, and who became afterwards the Head of a College and a Dean. He 'had his head so possest with a prince-like humour that ever after he did what then he acted, in his prodigal expences; so that the cost of a Sovereign ill befitting the purse of a subject, he died poor in prison, notwithstanding his great preferment'.

Palmer and most of his fellow actors also took part in the St. John's comedy *Hymenaeus* based on a story of the *Decameron*. This was one of a series of Cambridge Latin comedies in the last twenty years of the sixteenth century which pleased academic taste. Among these comedies, adapted more or less directly from Italian models, the most notable is *Laelia*, which was acted at Queens' College in 1595, though there is some evidence that suggests a much earlier first performance. The play is an adaptation, through the French version, of an Italian prose comedy *Gl'Ingannati* (the Cheated) acted at Siena. It is of special interest to readers of Shakespeare because it deals with the same story as forms the main plot of *Twelfth Night*. In the Cambridge play Laelia is Viola, Flaminius is Orsino, and Isabella is Olivia. Laelia has been the first love of Flaminius, and thus we are better prepared than in *Twelfth Night* for their final reunion. The love interest is delicately handled, but we miss the rich humours of the Shakespearian underplot with the figures of Sir Toby, Sir Andrew, and Malvolio.

While Cambridge was being entertained by Italianate comedy in Latin dress, Oxford was showing a more austere preference for neo-Senecan tragedy. Its chief representative was William Gager, who entered Christ Church from Westminster School in 1574, graduated in 1577, and became a Doctor of Civil Law in 1589. His first tragedy, *Meleager*, on the same subject as Swinburne's *Atalanta in Calydon*, was acted at Christ Church early in 1582 and revived three years later before the Chancellor of the University, the Earl of Leicester, who was accompanied by his nephew, Sir Philip Sidney.

Between the two productions of *Meleager* Gager had been called upon to furnish the plays for the entertainment in June 1583 of a foreign visitor to Oxford, the Prince Palatine of Poland, who was received with little less ceremony than the Queen herself in 1566.

> On the east gate wherat he entered stood a consort of musicians who for a long space made verie sweete harmonie, which could not but mooue and delight . . . All up the high street unto Saint Maries Church, on either side the waie, were decentlie marshalled scholers in their gownes and caps, bachelors and maisters in their habits and hoods. . . . From thense he marched to Christs Church, where he was whilest he abode in the universitie most honourablie interteined. And the first night being vacant, as in which he sought rather rest in his lodging than recreation in anie academicall pastimes, strange fire works were shewed in the great quadrangle, besides rockets and a number of such maner of deuises.

On the next evening, 11 June, a comedy by Gager, *Rivales*, was acted, but, though twice revived, it was never printed and has been lost. It was followed on 12 June by *Dido*, adapted by Gager on Senecan lines from Books I and IV of the *Aeneid*. It was staged with elaborate scenic effects, and is preserved in an ornamental manuscript, but it was probably hastily written for the occasion, and is the least original of Gager's plays. In a later tragedy based on the final episodes of the *Odyssey*, *Ulysses Redux*, acted early in 1592, he showed his ripest powers. With masterly technique he adapted to the limits of the Christ Church stage the story familiar to all in its noble epic breadth. *Ulysses Redux* would well have deserved the honour of being revived before the Queen when in September of the same year she paid a second visit to Oxford. But it was probably thought that the humours of *Rivales*, acted on 26 September, would be a greater diversion from the cares of State. More appropriate to the academic surroundings was the performance on the previous Sunday evening, the 24th, of *Bellum Grammaticale*, a dramatized version by Leonard Hutten, a distinguished member of Christ Church, of a popular humanist treatise which explained the irregularities of Latin grammar as the result of a civil war between the various parts of speech.

The presence of the Queen at these performances in Christ Church hall must have given special pleasure to Dr. Gager. The University authorities were at this time hostile to the professional touring companies and often paid them to go away. There was also a section of academic society that objected on various grounds to the amateur performances by the scholars. Their leader at this period was Dr. John Rainolds of Queen's College, afterwards President of Corpus Christi College. As an undergraduate he had played in the memorable performance of *Palamon and Arcyte* before Elizabeth in 1566, but he had become a fanatical opponent of acting in all its forms, and shortly before the royal visit of 1592 he had entered upon a controversy with Gager, in which he denounced college theatricals. In his reply Gager draws a distinction, which we would not endorse to-day, between the moral effects of amateur and professional acting, and proceeds to defend the former practice at the Universities.

> We do it . . . to practise our own style either in prose or verse; to be well acquainted with Seneca or Plautus; honestly to embolden our path; to try their [i.e. the scholars'] voices and confirm their memories; to frame their speech; to conform them to convenient action; to try what metal is in every one, and what disposition they are of; whereby never any one amongst us that I know was made the worse, many have been much the better.

As the reference to Seneca and Plautus, together with his own plays, proves, Gager is here thinking primarily of performances in Latin. And in December of this year we find the authorities of Cambridge, who had been asked to provide an English comedy to be acted by some of the scholars at the Christmas Court festivities, replying that 'we have no practice in this English vein . . . and do find our principal actors, whom we have of purpose called before us, very unwilling to play in English . . . English comedies, for that we have never used any, we presently have none'.

The Vice-Chancellor and his colleagues cannot have remembered *Gammer Gurtons Nedle*, and a further refutation of their statement was to be given in the last decade of Elizabeth's reign to which belong notable Cambridge comedies in English. In *Club-Law*, acted at Clare Hall probably in 1599–1600, the vernacular may have been used as intelligible to the leading citizens who according to a tradition were present at its performance. In any case it is a clever and virulent attack by 'gown' upon 'town'. The anonymous playwright (not improbably George Ruggle, a Fellow of Clare Hall, afterwards author of a Latin play, *Ignoramus*, which delighted James I) lays the scene in Athens, which represents Cambridge. The newly-elected Burgomaster (Mayor) announces that he will 'rout out' the academicians and arranges for the citizens to make an attack upon them with clubs. But his plans miscarry, the tables are turned upon him, and he and his chief supporters are sent to jail by the Rector (the Vice-Chancellor). The scholars are prohibited from having dealings with the leading citizens, and 'the town' is forced to beg for mercy. The piece is not so much a comedy as a succession of knock-down blows which are delivered with relentless vigour and precision.

Tudor academic comedy reaches its climax in the *Parnassus* trilogy, of which the Parts were successively acted at St. John's College, Cambridge, about 1598, 1600, and 1602. The author unfortunately cannot be identified. Only the third Part was published in 1606, with the title *The Return from Parnassus; or the Scourge of Simony*. The earlier pieces have been preserved in a a manuscript in the Bodleian Library and were printed in 1886 with the titles, *The Pilgrimage to Parnassus* and *Part I of the Return*.

The Pilgrimage is an allegory, in dramatic form, of the difficulties and temptations which the scholar has to encounter in the pursuit of learning. Two fellow students, Philomusus and Studiosus, are shown treading the academic path to Parnassus, meeting with trials on their way, but at last reaching the 'laurel mount'. In *Part I of the Return* the two students, having completed their University course, are driven to desperate shifts to make a living, Philomusus as a parish clerk and sexton, Studiosus as a private tutor. After further shifts at home and abroad they at last in *Part II of the Return* turn to the professional stage as a means of earning their bread. In a famous scene in Act IV they are tested in what would now be called an 'audition' by two of the leading members of Shakespeare's company, Burbage and Kempe. The latter in particular has a very mean opinion of their powers:

> *Kempe.* The slaves are somewhat proud and besides it is a good sport in a part to see them never speak in their walk, but at the end of the stage . . .
>
> *Burbage.* A little teaching will mend these faults, and it may be besides they will be able to pen a part.
>
> *Kempe.* Few of the University pen plays well . . . Why here's our fellow Shakespeare puts them all down, aye and Ben Jonson too. O that Ben Jonson is a pestilent fellow, he brought up Horace giving the poets a pill, but our fellow Shakespeare hath given him a purge that made him bewray his credit.

There is a reference here to a scene in Ben Jonson's *Poetaster* where, under the name of Horace, he gives pills to Crispinus (the rival dramatist, Marston) to make him disgorge his grandiloquent phrases. Unfortunately we can only speculate about the 'purge' that Shakespeare administered to Jonson. The academic dramatist is in any case expressing Kempe's views about his 'fellow's' triumph, not his own personal sympathies which were doubtless with 'Jonson's learned sock'. But these glimpses of professional actors and playwrights through the half-jealous, half-contemptuous eyes of the gifted Cambridge amateur are of unique interest. And he may well have been thinking of Shakespeare's prosperous fortunes, and of the grant-of-arms to his father when he puts into the mouths of the ill-fated pair of scholars the indignant cry:

England affords those glorious[1] vagabonds
That carried erst their fardels[2] on their backs
Coursers to ride on through the gazing streets,
Sooping it[3] in their glaring satin suits
And pages to attend their Masterships:
With mouthing words that better wits have framed,
They purchase lands, and now Esquires are named.

During the next half century under the Stuarts, plays were produced at Oxford or Cambridge that had more immediate and resounding success than the *Parnassus* group, but in its wealth of reference to contemporary academic, social, literary, and theatrical life the St. John's College trilogy makes to us to-day an abiding appeal.

[1] Swaggering. [2] Packs. [3] Sweeping along.

V

MASKS AND PAGEANTS

We have traced in preceding chapters the contributions made to Tudor drama by various types of amateur players and playwrights, including schoolmasters and their pupils, University 'dons' and undergraduates, and lawyers connected with the Inns of Court. All of these, in different fashions, leavened the native English dramatic forms with elements drawn from classical sources. We now turn to another dramatic or semi-dramatic type of entertainment which we also owe to amateurs of a different class, not concerned with education, academic or legal, but merely bent on 'fleeting the time carelessly' at Court or in great houses. Hence it is that the Mask is so peculiarly typical of the Renaissance age. Here are united the gay abandonment to the pleasure of the moment, the delight in spectacle and movement, the fanciful antiquarianism, the passion for self-expression through every kind of art. Thus the Mask, like Grand Opera to-day, was the distinctively international form of entertainment, and here England was indebted in the main, not to the ancient world but to contemporary France, Burgundy, and Italy.

The subject may be approached from two different but not mutually exclusive points of view. The scientific stage-historian will seek to give accurate interpretation as 'terms of art' to mask, momerie, disguising, intermezzo, triumph, and other related forms. He will trace their origins, their similarities and differences, the proportions in which they respectively mingle dance, music, spectacle, and speech. From extant examples, from descriptions by chroniclers, and from official account-books he will reconstruct, as far as possible, the evolution of the Mask.

For our present purpose, however, these more technical problems (which start even with the etymologies of 'momerie' and 'mask'), though kept in view, must be subordinated to a general consideration of the place of the Mask among the Tudor entertainments and its influence on the 'legitimate' drama. But the fact is to be briefly emphasized that it is of primitive origin.

> The story of the Masque begins with the dance of the seasonal festivals. Curiously enough the Court masquerade, that very sophisticated amusement of Renaissance society, was more primitive than the drama of the rough Elizabethan playhouse. From the beginning to the end of its history, the essence of the masque was the arrival of certain persons vizored and disguised to dance a dance or present an offering. This brings us very close indeed to ancient and almost world-wide ritual.[1]

Sir Edmund Chambers writes in somewhat similar strain, but he emphasizes one special feature.

> The mask is not primarily a drama; it is an episode in an indoor revel of dancing. Masked and otherwise disguised persons come, by convention unexpectedly, into the hall, as a compliment to the hosts or the principal guests. Often they bring them gifts; always they dance before them, and they invite them to join the dance . . . It is necessary to lay stress on the fact that the guests mingle with the maskers in the dance. Thus intimacy between performers and spectators differentiates the mask from the drama to the end.[2]

A mumming which has many of the features of the

[1] *The Court Masque*, by Enid Welsford, p. 2.
[2] *Elizabethan Stage*, vol. i, p. 149.

later mask, though there is no mention of dialogue, took place at Candlemas, 1577, in honour of Richard II:

> Ye comons of London made great sporte and solemnity to ye yong prince: for upon ye monday next before ye purification of our lady at night and in ye night were 130 men disguizedly aparailed and well mounted on horsebacke to goe on mumming to ye said prince, riding from Newgate through Cheape whear many people saw them with great noyse of minstralsye, trumpets, cornets and shawmes and great plenty of waxe torches lighted.

Arrayed as an emperor and a pope, with their respective trains, the mummers rode to Kennington, where they offered Richard lucky dice and golden gifts. He entertained them with wine, and bade the minstrels play. 'And ye prince and ye lordes dansed on ye one syde, and ye mummers on ye other a great while and then they drank and tooke their leaue'.

This elaborate mumming was at Candlemas, and it was on high days and holidays, Christmas, New Year, Twelfth Night, Shrovetide, and May-day that such revels customarily took place. They also became more and more a part of state ceremonies, coronations, visits of foreign princes and envoys, royal marriages, and similar events in the houses of the great nobles. But the wars abroad and at home in the fifteenth century left Englishmen little time for such 'toys', though Henry VI was welcomed back from France in 1431 with a series of allegoric and symbolical pageants.

It was in the Court of Burgundy, which during this period outshone for a time that of France, that fifteenth-century disguising rose to its greatest splendour. Philip the Good and Charles the Bold delighted in all forms of magnificent show, such as the Feast of the Pheasant at Lille, or the wedding ceremonies at Bruges which celebrated the union of Charles with Margaret of York, sister of Edward IV, in 1468. This marriage brought England into closer contact than before with the art and culture of the Low Countries.

But it was from the South that the main stimulus came that transformed the old disguising into the fully developed Mask. From the accession of Henry VIII to the outbreak of the Civil War the Mask, after the Italian model, was acclimatized and adapted in England. The division of the southern peninsula into so many small sovereign states, whatever political difficulties it brought, was highly favourable to the Arts. The ruling houses in Florence and Venice, Ferrara and Milan, Rome and Naples vied with one another in the sumptuousness of their ceremonial entertainments. And in contrast with the medieval chivalry of the Plantagenets and the Burgundians their pageantry was cast in the neo-classical mould of the Renaissance. Thus Lorenzo de Medici in Florence revived the 'triumphs' with which Roman generals had celebrated their victories. At Milan in 1489 the Duke, Gian Galeazzo, and his bride, Isabella of Aragon, were welcomed by a magnificent show, having as its chief feature a 'Paradiso' made by Leonardo da Vinci, with the seven planets, each of which, at the command of Jove, descended to offer a greeting to the bride. At Rome during the Carnival of 1521 Pope Leo X amused himself by watching masquerades and moriscoes, including one in which Venus and Cupid were prominent figures.

In France this passion for ceremonial revelry found also congenial soil, and with the coming of the Tudors it again took firm root in England. The parsimonious Henry VII, according to Bacon, 'was rather a princely and gentle spectator than seemed much to be delighted' with triumphs and disguises, but his wife, Elizabeth of York, had the fondness of her House for show and spectacle. She must have delighted in the most goodly and pleasant disguising with which the marriage of her eldest son, Prince Arthur, to Katharine of Aragon was celebrated in 1501 in Westminster Hall. On the first night three pageants were successively wheeled in. The first was a castle drawn by four great animals. Eight disguised ladies looked out of the windows, and on each of the four turrets sat a boy, dressed like a maiden, and singing. The second was a ship, having as passenger a lady dressed like a Spanish princess, and manned by a crew who 'in theyr counteynaunces, speeches and demeanour used and behaved themselves after the manner and guise of Mariners'. The ship having cast anchor, Hope and Desire descended and announced that they were ambassadors from knights of the Mount of Love, which formed the third pageant. This contained eight goodly knights who made an attack upon the castle, till the ladies yielded and came down to dance with them. During the dancing the pageants were removed, and after the disguisers had departed, some of the leading spectators descended into the hall and danced 'basse dances', which were measures of a slow and stately kind.

It is to be noted that here the disguising, in addition to pageantry and dancing, included something in the way of dramatic dialogue. Further disguisings took place on later evenings in Westminster Hall, and afterwards at Richmond. Here the pageant was in the form of a tower with two stories, in the upper part of which were eight disguised ladies, and in the lower eight knights. Before the latter descended to dance they let loose conies, or rabbits, which ran about the hall; the ladies let fly doves and other birds, and then came down to dance with the knights.

The untimely death of Prince Arthur, whose wedding had thus been joyously celebrated, left his younger brother Henry to succeed him as heir to the throne and as Katharine's husband. The accession in 1509 of this full-blooded, pleasure-loving sovereign, the very type in his younger days of a Renaissance prince, gave an unprecedented stimulus to all forms of revelry. And fortunately for our present purpose Edward Halle, the chief chronicler of Henry's reign, thought it more important to depict in glowing pages these courtly festivities, than to record events that would be of higher value in the eyes of a constitutional historian. It is Halle who singles out Twelfth Night, 1512, as the date of the first appearance of the Italian Mask in England:

> On the daie of the Epiphanie at night, the Kyng with XI other wer disguised, after the maner of Italie, called a maske, a thyng not seen afore in Englande, they were appareled in garmentes long and brode, wrought all with gold, with visers and cappes of gold and after the banket doen, these Maskers came in, with sixe gentlemen disguised in silke bearyng staffe torches, and desired the ladies to daunce, some were content, and some that knewe the fashion of it refused, because it was not a thyng commonly seen. And after thei daunced and commoned together, as the fashion of the Maskes is, thei toke their leave and departed, and so did the Quene, and all the ladies.

There has been much debate as to what the precise novelty was on this occasion to which Halle drew such pointed attention. Some have thought that he was referring to the long gowns and hats with hoods which contrasted with the shorter garments previously worn in Court disguisings. And there seems to be no doubt that there was such a change of costume. But the essential innovation, which took some of the ladies aback as a thing not commonly seen, was that the performers asked ladies among the spectators to dance with them. 'The disguising was essentially a piece played before an audience, in which only disguisers danced together, whereas in the masque, the masquers chose out ladies in the audience for their dancing partners.'[1]

In Wolsey the King found a minister of state who had as great a zest for princely pleasures as himself, and Cavendish, the Cardinal's gentleman-usher and biographer, is a rival to Halle in his famous description of the mask with which the King interrupted a banquet given by Wolsey.

> I have seen the King suddenly come thither in a mask, with a dozen of other maskers, all in garments like shepherds, made of fine cloth of gold and fine crimson satin paned, and caps of the same, with visors of good proportion of visnomy; their hairs and beards, either of fine gold wire or else of silver, and some being of black silk; having sixteen torch bearers, beside their drums, and other persons attending upon them, with visors, and clothed all in satin, of the same colours. And at his coming, and before he came into the hall, ye shall understand, that he came by water to the water gate, without any noise; where, against his coming, were laid charged many chambers, and at his landing they were all shot off, which made such a rumble in the air, that it was like thunder. It made all the noblemen, ladies, and gentlemen to muse what it should mean coming so suddenly, they sitting quietly at a solemn banquet. . . . Then immediately after this great shot of guns, the Cardinal desired the Lord Chamberlain and Comptroller, to look what this sudden shot should

[1] E. Welsford, *op. cit.*, p. 135.

mean, as though he knew nothing of the matter. They thereupon looking out of the windows into Thames, returned again, and showed him that it seemed to them there should be some noblemen and strangers arrived at his bridge, as ambassadors from some foreign prince.

The Lord Chamberlain went to meet them, and having conducted them into the presence of the Cardinal, acted as interpreter:

> Sir, forasmuch as they be strangers, and can speak no English, they have desired me to declare unto your Grace thus: they, having understanding of this your triumphant banquet, where was assembled such a number of excellent fair dames, could do no less, under the supportation of your good grace, but to repair hither to view as well their incomparable beauty, as for to accompany them at mumchance,[1] and then after to dance with them and so to have of them acquaintance.

The Cardinal having given his consent,

> Then the maskers went first and saluted all the dames as they sat, and then returned to the most worthiest, and there opened a cup full of gold with crowns, and other pieces of coin, to whom they set divers pieces to cast at. Thus in this manner perusing all the ladies and gentlewomen, and to some they lost, and of some they won. And thus done, they returned unto the Cardinal, with great reverence, pouring down all the crowns in the cup, which was about two hundred crowns. 'At all' quoth the Cardinal, and so cast the dice, and won them all at a cast; whereat was great joy made.

Then followed the Cardinal's failure to identify the disguised King; Henry's removal of his visor, and the new apparelling of the maskers for the second banquet where he presided under the cloth of estate. 'Thus

[1] A game of dice.

passed they the whole night with banqueting, dancing and other triumphant devices.'

This account is of special interest for more than one reason. In the first place Cavendish preserves for us the details that only an eye-witness could furnish. And in these details there is a remarkable mixture of the older and newer elements of the Mask. There are the traditional features—the vizards, the torches, the sport at 'mumchance' or dicing, first with the ladies, and then with the Cardinal in whose favour, as in that of Richard II in 1377, the dice were doubtless loaded. And on the other hand there is the novel practice of the maskers inviting the ladies 'to dance with them and so have of them acquaintance', though on this occasion before doing so they changed into fresh apparel.

When Shakespeare and his collaborators introduced this episode into the first Act of *King Henry VIII* they gave it a new and unhistorical significance by making Henry choose Anne Boleyn as his partner in the dance.

> *K. Hen.* The fairest hand I ever touch'd! O beauty
> Till now I never knew thee . . .
>   My lord chamberlain
> Prithee come hither. What fair lady 's that?
> *Cham.* An't please your grace, Sir Thomas Bullen's daughter,
> The Viscount Rochford, one of her highness' women.
> *K. Hen.* By heaven, she is a dainty one.—Sweetheart,
> I were unmannerly to take you out,
> And not to kiss you.

Dramatically this addition is, of course, justified, but for the student of the Tudor Mask nothing is needed to heighten the interest of Cavendish's own account. At a later time, however, after Wolsey's fall, Anne Boleyn, now Marchioness of Pembroke, did figure in a mask of historical importance during the meeting at Calais in 1532 of Henry and King Francis I. On this occasion the ladies for the first time, so far as is known, invited the gentlemen to dance.

> After Supper came in the Marchiones of Pembroke, with vii ladies in Maskyng apparel . . . these ladies were brought into the Chamber, with four damoselles apareled in Crimosyn sattyn, with Tabardes of fine Cipres: The lady Marques tooke the Frenche Kyng, and the Countes of Darby toke the Kyng of Naverr, and every Lady toke a lorde, and in daunsyng the Kyng of Englande toke awaie the ladies visers.

This is a sample of the ways in which the Mask, in its stricter sense, changed and developed. It assimilated features from the older disguising and the newer interlude, and it gradually became the recognized title for very varied shows and devices, including in different proportions spectacle, dancing, music, and dialogue. Halle's description of the entertainment given by Henry in 1527 to the French ambassadors in the great chamber of disguisings at Greenwich suggests a fixed *mise-en-scène* instead of pageants on wheels. After the first part of the show, 'at the nether ende, by lettyng doune of a courtaine, apered a goodly mount'. On this mount sat eight lords who descended to dance first with ladies in the audience and then with Princess Mary and seven of her ladies who came out of a cave. Afterwards the King and the Viscount of Touraine, with six other lords, put on masking apparel,

> greate, long, and large, after the Venicions fashion and over them great robes, and there faces were visard with beardes of gold: then with minstrelsie these viii noble personages entred and daunced long with the ladies, and when they had daunced there fyll, then the quene

plucked of the kynges visar, and so did the Ladies the visars of the other Lordes, and then all were knowen.

Here, as in the 1512 Epiphany mask, Halle makes special reference to the long Italian garments worn by the men, and their golden visors. It was Katharine who uncased Henry, and it must have been one of the last occasions when the royal pair joined in such gay pastime. For it was in this year 1527 that Henry began to make public his scruples about his marriage with his brother's former wife. The shadow was on the horizon that was henceforth to darken a reign that had been for nearly two decades a golden time of which the Mask was the fittingly joyous symbol.

During the brief reigns of Edward VI and of Mary, overclouded by religious and political strife, we depend for our knowledge of Court festivities chiefly on the accounts of the Revels Office and other manuscript documents. In 1550–1 there was a mask of Moors at Christmas, one of Irishmen on Twelfth Night, and of Irishwomen at Shrovetide. In 1552 on Twelfth Night an interlude, *Aesop's Crowe*, in which five actors represented birds, was followed by a dialogue of *Youth and Riches*, as to which of them was better. 'After some pretty reasoning there came in six champions, of either side', who fought, two to two, at barriers in the hall. The Christmastide festivities of 1551–2 and 1552–3 were marked by considerable friction between the Master of the Revels, Sir Thomas Cawarden and George Ferrers, a poet of some note, for whom the office of Lord of Misrule had been revived.[1] Cawarden made difficulties about meeting the extensive demands of Ferrers

[1] See below, p. 75.

for apparel and properties and reduced him on one occasion to signing himself 'the lorde Myserabell'. The chief show that he presented during the Christmas season of 1552–3 was an elaborate *Triumph of Venus and Mars* for which he gave detailed instructions in letters to Cawarden. The other entertainments of this season and later in 1553, were of a somewhat grotesque character, a mask of covetous men with long noses, a mask of cats, a mask of bagpipes, a mask of tumblers going upon their hands with their feet upward, and a mask of 'medyoxes', double-visaged, half man, half death. This was an ill-omened entertainment, with a young king in feeble health, and soon after the presentation of an equally inappropriate 'drunken mask' at Midsummer, he died.

Queen Mary had a more austere taste than her boy brother, and though, as has been seen, she gave liberal encouragement to Udall in his dramatic activities, she allowed the office of Lord of Misrule to lapse, and masks were a less notable feature in the Court entertainments. But they included in 1554–5 a mask of Mariners, of Hercules, of Venetian senators, and Turkish magistrates, and in April 1557 a mask of Almains, Pilgrims, and Irishmen.

Elizabeth inherited from both her parents a delight in every form of revelry tempered only by the economical spirit of her grandfather, Henry VII. There is a significant postscript to the Revels Accounts for 1559–60, the second year of her reign. 'Memorandum that the Chargies for the making of maskes cam never to so little a somme as they do this yere [i.e. £227 11*s.* 2*d.*] for the same did ever amount . . . heretofore to the somme of cccc^{li} alwaies when it was Leaste'. But if the entertainments were not as lavish as under Henry VIII, they were at least as frequent and more varied. It is noteworthy that the first mask at the court of the new Protestant queen, on Twelfth Night, 1559, was of a burlesque ecclesiastical type. It consisted, as a scandalized foreign observer relates, of 'a mummery performed after supper . . . of crows in the habits of Cardinals, of asses habited as Bishops, and of wolves representing Abbots', all elaborately costumed from the wardrobe of the Revels Office. Other masks at Court of about the same time, of Hungarians, of Turks, and of six Moors, gave the opportunity for the displaying of supposedly national costumes, though the accounts of the Revels Office show that the garments used in one mask were frequently 'translated' and adapted to the needs of another. A different variety of mask was that which presented persons belonging to a particular trade or avocation. Thus on Shrove Tuesday, 1559, there were one or more masks of Fishermen, Fisherwives, and Marketwives, and on 24 May, in a banquet house at Westminster, for the entertainment of the Duke of Montmorency, Constable of France, a mask of Astronomers, whose long robes of Turkey red were at a later date 'translated' into garments for a mask of eight clowns. On Shrove Tuesday, 1560, the mythological mask reappeared with Diana and Actaeon, attendant nymphs and huntsmen, torchbearers, and hounds.

As the Revels Accounts are missing for the period from Shrovetide 1560 to Christmas 1571, the detailed information about Court entertainments does not begin again till 1572. In that year, on 15 June, the Duke of Montmorency was again welcomed as ambassador of France with an elaborate mask at Whitehall, partly allegorical, celebrating the defeat of Discord and the triumph of Peace, partly classical, introducing a rock and fountain for Apollo and the nine Muses. For the preparation of this important entertainment several foreign artists were employed. Payments were made to 'Haunce Eottes' (Hans Eworth), a Flemish painter, for 'patternes', and to 'Petrucio' (Petruccio Ubaldini), an Italian of versatile talents, for his 'travell and paynes', while another Italian, Alfonso Ferrabosco, the musician, is the 'Mr. Alphonse', who had the 'apoyntment' of the proceedings.

Ubaldini's services were again called upon for the double mask of Amazons and of Knights with which on 11 January 1579 another French envoy, M. de Simier, was entertained. Both groups were preceded by 'one with A speach to the Quenes maiestie delivering A Table with writinges', which were Italian versions of the speeches made by Ubaldini.

Details of the Court masks during Elizabeth's later years, especially from 1589 when the Revels accounts are missing, become scanty. But it was not only at Whitehall or Hampton Court that Gloriana was the centre of brilliant masquerade. She delighted in the 'progresses' of which her visits to Cambridge in 1564 and to Oxford in 1566 were early examples, and which included more extensive journeys to the country seats of great nobles or to leading provincial cities. Her hosts vied with one another in providing all manner of shows and spectacles for her amusement. The most famous of these were the 'princely pleasures' provided for her by the Earl of Leicester on her visit to Kenilworth in July 1575. No mask, however, was performed on this occasion, though a costly one had been prepared.

In August 1578, when Elizabeth visited Norwich, which was one of the chief dramatic centres outside of the capital, an 'excellent princely maske' by Henry Goldingham was brought before her after supper. It was 'of gods and goddesses, both strangely and richly apparelled'. Mercury first appeared, and was followed by Jupiter and Juno, Mars and Venus, Apollo and Pallas, Neptune and Diana, walking in pairs, preceded by torchbearers. Cupid came last, by himself. After a prologue by Mercury, Jupiter and Juno, followed by the other deities, made speeches to the Queen and offered her presents. At the end, 'with the reste of the maske' they 'marched aboute the chamber againe, and then departed in like manner as they came in'. Here are many of the characteristic features of the mythological mask, but there is no mention of dancing at the close. The townsfolk, who were the performers, no doubt kept at a respectful distance from the lords and ladies in the royal train.

It has been pointed out that there are striking resemblances between this Norwich entertainment and the mask in celebration of Sir Henry Unton's wedding in 1580, as represented in a picture in the National Portrait gallery. The maskers walk in pairs, separated by Cupids, five white and five black, as torchbearers, with Mercury and Diana in front, and a drummer at the head of the procession.

A later wedding mask which Elizabeth honoured with her presence on 16 June 1600, was to celebrate the marriage of one of her maids of honour, Anne, daughter of Elizabeth Lady Russell, to Henry, Lord Herbert. The mask, which took place after supper, at the house of Lord Cobham, introduced eight Muses, dancing to the music of Apollo, and seeking their ninth sister. An eye-witness wrote:

Delicate it was to see eight ladies so pretily and richly

Wedding Mask of Sir Henry Unton,
with other scenes from his life
From a painting in the National Portrait Gallery

> attired, Mrs. Fetton leade; and after they had donne all their own ceremonies, these eight ladie maskers chose eight ladies more to dawnce the measures. Mrs. Fetton went to the Queen, and woed her to dawnce. Her Majesty asked what she was? *Affection*, she said. *Affection* said the Queen, is false. Yet her Majestie rose and dawnced.

Could there be a more memorable close to these brief annals of Tudor disguisings and masks than the picture of the elderly Virgin Queen, with a gibe against Affection on her lips, rising to dance with Mary Fitton, in whom some have seen the 'dark lady' of Shakespeare's Sonnets?

VI

THE CHILDREN'S COMPANIES AND LYLY'S COURT-COMEDIES

THE organization of entertainments, dramatic and semi-dramatic, on the scale to which they attained in the Tudor Courts could not be left entirely in the hands of amateurs, though from their ranks was selected a Lord of Misrule to superintend the Christmas Revels. As the chronicler, Stowe, relates:

> There was in the feast of Christmas in the King's house, wheresoever he was lodged, a Lord of Misrule or Master of Merry Disports: and the like had ye in the house of every nobleman of honour or good worship, were he spiritual or temporal. Among the which the Mayors of London and either of the Sheriffs had their several Lords of Misrule . . . These Lords beginning their rule on Allhallows eve, continued the same til the morrow after the feast of the Purification, commonly called Candlemas-day.

There were many variants of the title of this functionary; Abbot of Misrule, Christmas Lord or Prince; in Scotland, Abbot of Unreason; at Gray's Inn (as has been seen) Prince of Purpoole, and at Merton College, Oxford, King of Beans. The 'Lord', however, under any title, and in any place, seems not to have been the 'producer' of the festivities in the modern technical sense, but a mock dignitary, with the appurtenances and trappings of royalty, who formed the centre of the revels.

In the household accounts of Henry VII a Lord of Misrule is mentioned for nearly every Christmas of his reign, with an annual fee of £6 13*s*. 4*d*. The custom was continued, with a gradually increasing fee, under

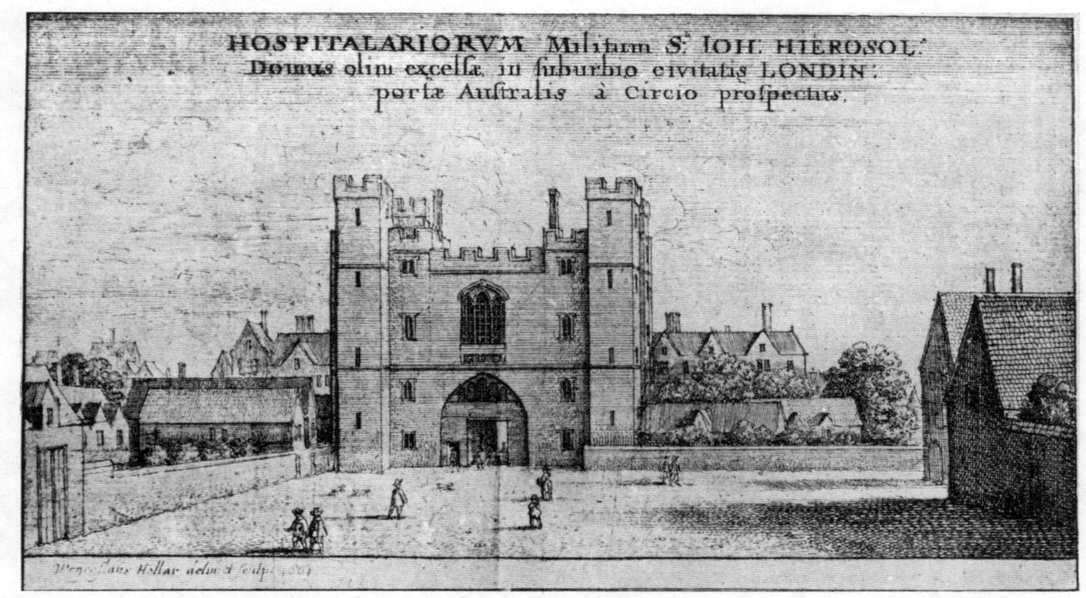

St. John's Gate

South entrance to the Hospital of St. John of Jerusalem, the seat of the Revels Office from 1560 to 1608

From Dugdale's *Monasticon*

Henry VIII, though after 1520 we are without documentary details except for 1534. The most notable holder of this temporary office was, as mentioned above, George Ferrers, the poet, one of the contributors to the *Mirror for Magistrates*, who was 'Lord' for Christmas 1551–2 and 1552–3. With the growth of the power of the Master of the Revels, a Lord of Misrule at Court became superfluous and under Mary and Elizabeth he disappeared.

Like the Lord of Misrule the Master of the Revels had at first been an *ad hoc* functionary. The earliest mention of the post is in a document of 31 December 1494. Its duties were administrative, and the temporary holders were assisted by a permanent official who belonged to the establishment of the Wardrobe.

> It was his business [as Sir Edmund Chambers has summed it up] to carry into effect the general directions of the Master; to obtain stuffs from mercers or from the Wardrobe itself, and ornaments from the Jewel House and the Mint; to engage architects, carpenters, painters, tailors, and embroiderers; to superintend the actual performances in the banqueting-hall or the tilt-yard, and attempt to preserve the costly and elaborate pageants from the rifling of the guests; to have the custody of dresses, visors, and properties; and finally, to render accounts and obtain payment for expenses from the Exchequer.

In March 1545 the permanent office of Master of the Revels was created, and Sir Thomas Cawarden of the King's privy chamber was appointed by patent the first holder of the post. He had under him, as the activities of the office grew, various subordinate officers, a Clerk Comptroller, and a Yeoman. Two years after Cawarden's appointment, in 1547, he made the dissolved Priory of Blackfriars the head-quarters of the office of the Revels, and it remained there during the reigns of Edward VI and Mary. On his death in August 1559 he was succeeded by Sir Thomas Benger, under whom the office was removed to the late Hospital of St. John of Jerusalem in Clerkenwell. After Benger's death in the summer of 1572, there was a vacancy in the Mastership, the duties of which were discharged by Thomas Blagrove, the Clerk, until Christmas, 1579. He was anxious to be appointed Master, but the post was conferred upon Edmund Tilney, who had a long tenure of the office till his death in August 1610, though after the accession of James I, his nephew, Sir George Buc, who had secured the reversion of the post, acted as his deputy. At an early period of Tilney's Mastership, the powers of the office were greatly extended by a patent dated 24 December 1581. The Master was authorized to press workmen, and to take 'stuff, ware, or merchandise' on payment of a reasonable price. Furthermore he was empowered

> to warne commaunde and appointe . . . all and euery plaier or plaiers with their playmakers, either belonginge to any noble man or otherwise, bearinge the name or names of vsinge the facultie of playmakers or plaiers of Comedies, Tragedies, Enterludes or what other showes soever, from tyme to tyme and at all tymes to appeare before him with all suche plaies, Tragedies, Comedies or showes as they shall haue in readines or meane to sett forth, and them to presente and recite before our said Servant or his sufficient deputie, whom wee ordeyne appointe and aucthorise by these presentes of all suche showes, plaies, plaiers and playmakers, together with their playing places, to order and reforme, auctorise and put downe, as shalbe thought meete or vnmeete vnto himself or his said deputie in that behalfe.

In this somewhat surprising way, by virtue of some of the clauses of a patent of remarkably diversified scope, the Master of the Revels became the official censor of the drama and the theatre. A lay authority took over a function which in the medieval period had been exercised by the Church. And in principle the new arrangement has lasted to our own day. For the Master of the Revels was attached to the Lord Chamberlain's branch of the Royal Household and though he has disappeared, his duties as Censor are now mainly exercised by another official of the Lord Chamberlain's department, the Examiner of plays. To-day his chief concern is with offences against morals. The Tudor, and still more the Stuart, Masters, while careless, according to modern standards, of the proprieties, had often the nicest scruples about expressions, including all forms of oaths, in any way 'touching on religion or policy'. There are no more interesting dramatic documents than the manuscripts of plays still extant with the autograph signatures of one or other of the Masters of the Revels 'allowing' them for performance, or indicating the necessary 'reformations'.

In organizing the entertainments at Court, the Masters of the Revels, from the early Tudor period, had the advantage of being able to rely partly on professional or semi-professional organizations attached to the Royal Household. There was a company of players of the King's Interludes, which under Henry VIII numbered eight, and which included Richard Gibson, who also was a Revels officer and kept accounts, still preserved, of many of the Court festivities. But a more important part in the entertainments under the Tudor sovereigns was played by the Gentlemen and Children of the

Chapel Royal. The 'fellowship of the Chapel' existed primarily to celebrate divine service for the Royal Household. Under the Dean and the Subdean its leading member was the Master of the Children, who was responsible for their musical training. The earliest holder of the office appears to have been John Plummer, 1444–55. Of the two Masters in the reign of Henry VII, Lawrence Squier, 1486–93, and William Newark, little is known. But William Cornish, who succeeded Newark late in 1509 and remained Master till his death in 1523, stimulated the dramatic activities of the Children and played a principal part in the organization of the Court entertainments.

The *Household Book* of King Henry VIII contains such entries as on 4 January 1517:

> Item to Mr Cornisshe and the Children of the Chapell that playd afore the King in reward vi$^{li.}$ xiij$^{s.}$ iiij$^{d.}$

or on 1 April 1520:

> Item to master Cornisshe for playing of ij enterludes w^{t} his Children afore ye King at grenewich xiii$^{li.}$ vj$^{s.}$ viij$^{d.}$

which are typical of others between 1511 and 1521.

The year 1517 was one of marked activity for Cornish and the Children of the Chapel. In addition to the payment on 4 January quoted above, there is another to him on 8 March for a play acted on Shrove Tuesday, 24 February. And between these dates, on Twelfth Night, there was a performance of a pageant *The Gardyn de Esperans* described by Halle. The *Household Book* records that £133 19*s.* 0*d.* was spent upon it and also that an explanatory prologue was spoken by Cornish.

> Of which garden Master Cornish showed by speech the effect and intent imparelled like a stranger in a gown of red sarcanet and a coat of arms on him, his

horse trappered with blue sarcenet, and so declaring his purpose.'

It is right that Cornish's claim to an important place in the history of the Chapel Royal and of the revels at the court of Henry VIII should have been vindicated. But there is nothing either in the documents or in such of his writings as can be identified to uphold the further claim that has been made on his behalf to be the author of plays ascribed on good grounds to Heywood or to Rastell.

Cornish was succeeded by William Crane, 1523–45, and Crane by Richard Bower, 1545–61. To the latter has been conjecturally assigned the tragi-comedy on a classical subject, *Apius and Virginia*, of which the author is R. B. But there is no reference on the title-page to the Children, and the play though entered on the Stationers' Register, 1567–8, was not published till 1575.

We are on surer ground with the next Master, Richard Edwardes, though he held this office only from October 1561 till October 1566, when he died. We may be grateful for the full title-page of his surviving play: 'The excellent Comedie of two the moste faithfullest Freends, Damon and Pithias. Newly Imprinted, as the same was shewed before the Queenes Maiestie, by the Children of her Graces Chappell . . . Made by Maister Edwards, then beynge Maister of the Children. 1571.' This was in all probability the 'tragedy' performed by the Children of the Chapel, as the Revels accounts record, at Court during the Christmas season 1564–5. It might, in the loose terminology of the time, be described either as a comedy or a tragedy for with the grave and moving story of Damon and Pithias, one of whom imperils his life for the other, Edwardes combines the realistically humorous episodes of Grim, the collier of Croydon, and the saucy varlets, Will and Jack. He was an Oxford man, successively of Corpus and of Christ Church, and it was probably the success of *Damon and Pithias* which led to his being invited to write *Palamon and Arcyte*, for performance before the Queen during her visit to the University in the summer of 1566, as related in a previous chapter. But for the loss of this play, and his premature death so soon afterwards, Edwardes would stand higher among the earlier Elizabethan dramatists than has always been recognized.

His successor was William Hunnis, who held the post for thirty years, till his death in June 1597. Several volumes of his religious and moral verse, with quaint alliterative titles, such as *A Handful of Honnisuckles* and *Seven Sobbes of a Sorrowful Soule for Sinne*, are extant. And he must have written plays, for an admiring friend speaks of

> Thy Enterludes, thy gallant Layes, thy Rond'letts and
> thy Songes.

The attempt, however, by his enthusiastic modern biographer, Mrs. C. C. Stopes, to identify *Godly Queen Hester* and *Jacob and Esau* as plays from his pen is not convincing. It is reasonable to suppose that some of his 'enterludes' were acted at Court by his boys, but in any case his long mastership is notable in various ways. Soon after his appointment in 1569, in a pamphlet *The Children of the Chapel Stript and Whipt*, a bitter attack was made upon his boys:

> Even in her maiesties chappel do these pretty vpstart youthes profane the Lordes Day by the lascivious writhing of their tender limbs and gorgeous decking of their apparell, in feigning bawdie fables gathered from the idolatrous heathen poets.

Some vivid light is thrown upon the relations between the Master and the Children and the conditions in which they performed their varied duties by a petition presented by Hunnis in November 1583, from which the following are extracts:

> Maye it please your honores, William Hunnys, M^{r} of the Children of hir highnes Chappell, most humble beseecheth to consider of these fewe lynes. First, hir Maiestie alloweth for the dyett of xij children of hir sayd Chappell daylie vi^{d} a peece by the daye, and xl^{li} by the yeare for theyre aparrell and all other furneture.
>
> Agayne there is no fee allowed neyther for the m^{r} of the sayd children nor for his ussher, and yet neuertheless is he constrayned, over and besydes the ussher still to kepe bothe a man servant to attend vpon them and lykewyse a woman seruant to wash and kepe them cleane.
>
> Also there is no allowance for the lodginge of the sayd chilldren, such tyme as they attend vppon the Courte, but the m^{r} to his greate charge is dryuen to hyer chambers both for himself, his usher chilldren and servantes . . .
>
> In tender consideracion whereof, might it please your honores that the sayde allowaunce of vj^{d} a daye apeece for the childrens dyet might be reserued in hir Maiesties coffers during the tyme of theyre attendaunce. And in liew thereof they to be allowed meate and drinke within this honorable householde for that I am not able vppon so small allowaunce eny longer to beare so heauie a burden.

It is impossible not to add to Sir Edmund Chambers's comment:

> The actual request made by Hunnis seems a modest one. He seems to have thought that for his boys to have the run of their teeth at the tables of Whitehall would be a better bargain then the board-wages of 6*d*. a day. Doubtless he knew their appetites.

His request does not appear to have been granted.

Was it this dissatisfaction with the conditions of his post that had apparently led Hunnis from 1576–7 to 1579–80 to discharge his duties through a deputy, Richard Farrant, Master of the Children of Windsor? Farrant had been a Gentleman of the Chapel from 1553 to 1564, when he became Master of the Choir of St. George's Chapel. Under his direction the Children of Windsor gave a series of performances at Court from February 1567 to December 1575, including plays on classical subjects, *Ajax and Ulysses*, *Quintus Fabius*, *King Xerxes*. On 6 January 1577, another play on a classical theme, *Mutius Scaevola*, was performed at Court by the Children of Windsor and the Chapel. Farrant had in 1570 been reappointed a Gentleman of the Chapel Royal, and in the Revels Accounts for 1576–7 till 1579–80 he appears as Master of the Children of the Chapel, though apparently as deputy for Hunnis. Farrant in 1577, and perhaps in the following years, had made a combined company out of the two choirs with which he was associated. All this was connected with his important enterprise (first made known through the researches of Professor Feuillerat in 1912) of taking a lease on 26 December 1576 of some of the old Priory buildings in Blackfriars from Sir William More, and converting them into the first *Blackfriars* Theatre. Here the Children of the Chapel gave public performances.

At this point it is necessary to turn to another company of children, those belonging to the choir or song school of St. Paul's Cathedral. This is distinct from the grammar school, also connected with the Cathedral, which was reorganized by Dean Colet in 1512, and which since 1883 on a new site in Hammersmith is still a centre of humanist teaching. The boys of the grammar school, purely amateurs, took their share, as has been seen, in the acting of plays in Henry VIII's reign. But under Elizabeth it appears to have been the boys of the choir school who came to the front as actors for her entertainment. Their Master from 1557 to 1582 was Sebastian Westcott, who, in spite of his leanings to 'Papistrie', kept the Queen's favour, and appeared with his boys at Court in twenty-seven plays. After his death, under this successor, Thomas Giles, they appear to have followed the example of the Children of the Chapel, and to have joined them in acting at the Blackfriars theatre. For the play of *Campaspe* by John Lyly, published in 1584, has on the title-page of what was probably the first of three issues in that year, the statement that it was played before the Queen 'by her Maiesties Children and the Children of Poules', and it contains a double set of Prologues and Epilogues 'at the Blackfriars', and 'at Court'. As the amateur pupils of Nicholas Udall had the distinction of first presenting *Ralph Roister Doister*, which marks the beginning of Elizabethan comedy, in the sense previously explained,[1] so to the semi-professional Children fell the higher honour of bringing before the Court and the wider public of the *Blackfriars* the first, and also the second, of the comedies with which John Lyly inaugurated the golden period of the Elizabethan theatre.

Lyly was setting a precedent, which has been conspicuously followed in our own day, of exploiting for the stage a reputation already made as a novelist. Born about 1554 in Kent, probably at Canterbury, he had been educated at Magdalen College, Oxford, taking his M.A. in 1575. Within a few years of his arrival

[1] See above, p. 25.

in London, he leapt into fame with the publication of his *Euphues* in 1578, followed in 1580 by its second part, *Euphues and his England.* These books at once became 'best sellers' both through their subject-matter and their style. They were novels with an edifying purpose, concerned with love, friendship, and morals and making a special appeal to women. The didactic element was more prominent in *Euphues*, while in its sequel there is a closer approach (as Professor R. W. Bond, the editor of the Oxford *Complete Works of John Lyly*, has shown) to the modern novel of manners, the 'romance of polite society'. Hence this second part includes a special dedication to the 'ladies and gentlemen of England':

> It resteth Ladies, that you take the paines to read it, but at such times, as you spend in playing with your little Dogges, and yet will I not pinch you of that pastime, for I am content that your Dogges lye in your laps, so *Euphues* may be in your hands, that when you shall be wearie in reading of the one, you may be ready to sport with the other: or handle him as you doe your Iunckets, that when you can eate no more, you tye some in your napkin for children, for if you be filled with the first part, put the second in your pocket for your wayting Maydes: *Euphues* had rather lye shut in a Ladyes casket, then open in a Schollers studie.

This passage, though quoted for its substance, may serve to illustrate some, though not all, of the characteristics of the style of Lyly's novel which even more than its subject, caught the ear of the time, and added 'Euphuism' as a permanent, though often incorrectly used, term to our English vocabulary. The basis of the style consists in its accumulation of balanced and antithetical clauses, e.g. 'your Dogges lye in your laps, so *Euphues* may be in your hands', 'rather lye shut in a

Ladyes casket, then open in a Schollers studie'. And this antithetical balance is driven home by an elaborate system of alliteration, partly within the single clause, e.g. *l*ye . . . *l*aps, *l*ye . . . *L*adyes, partly linking clause to clause, e.g. 'in *r*eading . . . be *r*eady', '*s*hut . . . *S*chollers *s*tudie'. Other features of the style were a prodigal use of similes, drawn largely from a purely fictitious natural history, and the constant repetition of rhetorical questions. Lyly did not invent this style. It had in its features of the 'alto estilo' of the Spaniard, Antonio de Guevara, and of the conceits of the Italian imitators of Petrarch. Lord Berners and Sir Thomas North had successively translated Guevara's *Diall for Princes*, and in 1576 George Pettie in his collection of stories from Italian originals, *The Petite Pallace of Pettie his Pleasure*, had anticipated many of the characteristic devices of Euphuism. But it was Lyly who made it 'the rage'.

And what is of special import from our point of view here is that Lyly the novelist is half-way to Lyly the dramatist. As one of his most recent critics has said:

> All through the book, whether the scene is laid in Naples or on board ship, or on the journey from Dover to London, Lyly's treatment of his material is that of a dramatist. Never a detailed description of his setting or his characters, never an explanation of the psychology of his puppets, except what is brought in in conversation. The rest might well be a series of stage directions.

And it was probably the triumphant success of his prose style in his novel that led Lyly to retain it for the purposes of dramatic dialogue when he turned to the stage, and thus fortunately to endow English comedy with an instrument immeasurably more flexible and delicate than the rhyming metres which, except in Gascoigne's version of *Gli Suppositi*, it had hitherto employed.

When Lyly published *Euphues and his England* in 1580, he was already in touch with theatrical affairs, for he dedicates the book to his 'very good lord and master', Edward de Vere, Earl of Oxford, who was Burleigh's son-in-law and Lord Chamberlain. As Oxford was included by Francis Meres in his *Wit's Treasury* (1598) among 'the best for comedy among us', he must have been a playwright, though no extant piece bears his name, and it has been left to a coterie of to-day to put him forward as a rival to Francis Bacon for the authorship of Shakespeare's plays. He had from 1580 two theatrical companies in his service, one of adult players, the other of boys who probably belonged to his domestic chapel. The Treasurer of the Chamber in his account specifies payments to John Lyly for performance by the Earl of Oxford's servants on 1 January and 3 March 1584, which correspond with the New Year's day and the Shrove Tuesday mentioned on the title-pages of *Campaspe* and *Sapho and Phao* respectively. It seems therefore that Oxford's boys had joined with the Children of the Chapel and the Children of Paul's in a company which acted at the *Blackfriars* and at Court, and that for this company Lyly, who was in the Earl's service, wrote his first two plays. In the spring of 1584 Sir William More resumed possession of the Blackfriars premises, and they could no longer be used as a theatre. But Lyly, as the title-pages of his plays prove, continued to write for the Paul's boys. *Gallathea*, *Endimion*, *Midas*, *Mother Bombie*, *Love's Metamorphosis* were all, on this evidence, played by the Children of Paul's, the three first, at any rate, before the Queen. They cannot be exactly dated but they fall between the Christmas season of 1584–5 and 1590, when 'the Plaies in Paules' were dissolved till the end of the century. *The Woman in the Moon*, Lyly's only verse play, was acted before the Queen, but the performers are not mentioned, and it was probably written later than the others and for another company.

It will be seen that the conditions under which Lyly's plays were produced helped to give them their special character. They were written (with probably one exception) for boys, to be performed before the select audiences of the Court or the *Blackfriars*. Hence they did not aim at the highly coloured effects, or deal with the violent passions and 'moving accidents' which formed the staple of the entertainment by the adult companies at the new public theatres. Lyly's comedies reflected the atmosphere, the interests, the modes of the Court society of his day. The dialogue is a heightened form of the conversation at its best and its wittiest of the gallants and fair ladies who composed Gloriana's brilliant train. In his plays women meet men on equal terms, and it is only when such a relation has been established between the sexes that comedy of the higher type can come into being.

The Queen herself led the fashion of an enthusiasm for classical lore, and the titles of Lyly's plays show that it was to Greek mythology and legend that he went for most of his subjects. In *Campaspe* he even touches on the sphere of Greek history for he introduces Alexander the Great, with his generals, and a group of Athenian philosophers, headed by Plato, Aristotle, and Diogenes. The cynic in his tub plays a game of repartee with Alexander, which is an example of how Lyly could at will simplify his style and turn it to the cut-and-thrust of rapid stage dialogue (II. ii):

Alex. If Alexander have any thing that may pleasure Diogenes let me know, and take it.

Diog. Then take not from me, that you cannot give me, the light of the world.

Alex. What dost thou want?

Diog. Nothing that you have.

Alex. I have the world at command.

Diog. And I in contempt.

Alex. Thou shalt live no longer than I will.

Diog. But I will die, whether you will or no.

Alex. How should one learn to be content?

Diog. Unlearn to covet.

Alex. Hephaestion, were I not Alexander, I would wish to be Diogenes.

One can easily imagine how the 'Children' would enjoy acting such a scene, or playing the parts of the quick-tongued servants of the philosophers.

But the main interest, which gives the play its title, lies in the rivalry between Alexander and the painter, Apelles, for the love of the beautiful Theban captive Campaspe. The scene in which the King confesses his passion to his chief general, Hephaestion, and is rebuked by him, illustrates the more Euphuistic elements in Lyly's dramatic style (III. ii):

Alex. And sith thou hast been always partaker of my triumphs, thou shalt be partaker of my torments. I love, Hephaestion, I love! I love Campaspe, a thing far unfit for a Macedonian, for a King, for Alexander . . .

Heph. I can not tell, Alexander, whether the report be more shameful to be heard, or the cause sorrowful to be believed . . . O Alexander, that soft and yielding mind should not be in him, whose hard and unconquered heart hath made so many yield. But you love, ah grief! but whom? Campaspe, ah shame! a maid forsooth unknown, unnoble, and who can tell whether immodest? Whose eyes are framed by art to enamour, and whose heart was made by nature to enchant. Ay, but she is beautiful;

yea but not therefore chaste; ay but she is comely in all parts of the body: yea, but she may be crooked in some part of the mind: ay, but she is wise, yea but she is a woman! Beauty is like the blackberry which seemeth red, when it is not ripe, resembling precious stones that are polished with honey, which the smoother they look, the sooner they break.

After some charming scenes in the studio where Apelles is painting Campaspe, and where the beginnings of art-jargon are first heard on the English stage, Alexander shows himself magnanimous, and bestows the maid on Apelles who has won her heart. If *Campaspe* was Lyly's first play he showed by his deft interlacing of the different threads in the plot that he was a born dramatist.

Similar characteristics of style and technique are to be found in the three plays of a more mythological type, *Sapho and Phao*, *Endimion*, and *Midas*. Each takes a well-known classical legend, adapts it to stage conditions, and interweaves with it subsidiary lighter episodes. About their merits as delicately fashioned court-comedies there can be no question. But they raise a problem to which different critics have given very varied solutions. Beneath the seeming innocence of their surface do they contain daring references to personages and events of the day? Does the mutual passion of Sapho, the princess of Syracuse, and the handsome ferryman, quenched later by the jealousy of Venus, allegorize the relations between Elizabeth and her French suitor, the Duke of Alençon? Is Endimion, hopelessly in love with the moon-goddess, Cynthia, a picture of the Earl of Leicester, fruitlessly aspiring to the hand of the Virgin Queen? And are the other chief characters in the same play, Tellus and Dipsas, Eumenides and

Corsites, modelled upon notables of Gloriana's Court, though commentators may not agree in their selection of the prototypes? It must be confessed that the game of identification is tempting, though Sir Edmund Chambers provides a 'cooling-card' when he declares that he finds no conviction in the attempts of various scholars 'to trace Elizabeth's politics and amours in the play. If Lyly had meant half of what they suggest, he would have ruined his career in her service at the outset'. But even if we rule out any allegorical intention in *Sapho and Phao* and *Endimion*, it is scarcely possible not to identify Midas, King of Phrygia, who has the fatal gift of turning all that he touches into gold, with Philip of Spain to whom the mines of the New World were to prove a ruinous treasure. And the island Kingdom of Lesbos that he seeks in vain to subdue must be England (III. i.).

> A bridge of gold did I mean to make in that island where all my navy could not make a breach. Those islands did I long to touch, that I might turn them to gold, and my self to glory. But unhappy Midas, who by the same means perisheth himself, that he thought to conquer others: being now become a shame to the world, a scorn to that petty prince, and to thy self a consumption. A petty prince, Midas? No, a prince protected by the gods, by nature, by his own virtue, and his subjects' obedience.

In such thinly disguised references to the overthrow of the Armada and to the divine favour bestowed on Elizabeth, Lyly was on safer ground than in veiled allusions to her love-affairs. And to-day we can, if we will, give a new turn to his dramatic application of the legend of Midas. We may see in it an anticipation of the fates of the countries that have brought catastrophe on themselves and on the world by hoarding in their bank-vaults immense stores of sterilized gold.

Three other plays, *Gallathea*, *Love's Metamorphosis*, and *The Woman in the Moon*, though they have mythological features, are akin in their sylvan background and their filmy texture to the pastoral dramas of Italy. They are set respectively in north Lincolnshire, in Arcadia, and in Utopia, but these are merely variant names of an enchanted borderland in which gods and goddesses intermingle with shepherds and foresters, nymphs and country maidens. Here Gallathea and Phillida, to escape sacrifice to the sea-monster Agar, are disguised by their shepherd fathers as boys, and are inflamed by a mutual passion which can only be satisfied when Venus undertakes to turn one of them into a real boy at the church-door. Here three nymphs of Ceres, disdaining the suit of three enamoured foresters, are metamorphosed by Cupid into a rock, a rose, and a bird till they relent. Here Pandora, the woman created by Nature at the petition of the Utopian shepherds, is subjected in turn to the influence of each of the seven planets and creates jealousy and discord till Nature translates her to a place in the moon, with the shepherd, who had been her husband, as her attendant man in the moon.

It is a great change from the mythological and pastoral plays to *Mother Bombie*, a comedy in the tradition of Plautus and Terence, in which scheming and avaricious old men are outwitted in match-making by the younger generation, with the help of nimble-witted servants. The two editions of the play in 1594 and 1598 state that it was acted by the Children of Paul's but do not name the author. It was first assigned to Lyly by the bookseller, Edward Blount, when he included it in 1632 in his edition of *Six Court Comedies*. It has been accepted by later editors, but the question has recently been raised whether it is really from Lyly's pen, and the evidence is not conclusive.

But Blount's edition raises another problem of wider interest. Plays written for performance by the Children would naturally take advantage of their musical talents. And in the stage directions or dialogue of the quarto editions of Lyly's plays there is the indication of thirty-two songs. Except however for two snatches in *The Woman in the Moon* the words of the songs are missing in the earliest editions. Blount in 1632 supplied the words of twenty-one which were long accepted as, without doubt, by Lyly. Early in the present century, however, their genuineness was challenged, and a long sustained discussion has followed. Somewhat detailed questions of vocabulary and style are involved, and the last word has probably not yet been said. But, on the whole, the debate has recently turned more in Lyly's favour than at an earlier stage, and we are not as yet compelled to withhold from him the credit of such delightful lyrics as

> Cupid and my Campaspe played
> At cards for kisses; Cupid paid.

and

> What bird so sings, yet so does wail?
> O, 'tis the ravished nightingale.

With Lyly's double success as novelist and playwright he might well have expected advancement at Court, and from letters still extant that he wrote to Sir Robert Cecil and the Queen between the end of 1597 and the beginning of 1601 it is evident that he got a Household post, and was encouraged about 1588 to hope for the reversion of the Mastership of the Revels, to which however Buc was preferred. One of Lyly's petitions to the Queen is written in his characteristic style:

I was entertayned your Maiesties servant by your owne gratious ffavour, strenghthened with condicions, that I should ayme all my courses att the Revels (I dare not saye with a promise, butt a hopeffull Item, of the Reversion); ffor the which, theis tenn yeares, I haue attended, with an vnwearyed patience, and I knowe not whatt crabb tooke mee ffor an oyster that in the middest of the svnn-shine of your gratious aspect, hath thrust a stone betwene the shelles, to eate mee alyve, that onely lyve on dead hopes.

Lyly seems at last, as he again characteristically put it, to have got something not out of 'the Revels', but out of 'the Rebels'—the property forfeited by those engaged in the Essex conspiracy of 1601. But his worldly hopes had been, in the main, disappointed when he died in November 1606, and though Blount in 1632 blazoned him as 'the onely Rare Poet of that Time: The Witie, Comicall, Facetiously-Quicke and vnparalelled: John Lilly', his reputation as a dramatist suffered a swift eclipse. But the wheel has again turned, and the last half century has increasingly recognized his achievement as a creator of a distinctive type of high comedy in prose and his many-sided influence on the art and style of Shakespeare. The reader of the 'court-comedies' may with advantage turn to Professor Warwick Bond's pages on 'What Shakespeare owes to Lyly',[1] and starting from this basis seek to investigate on his own account the debt of the master-dramatist to the playwright who turned to such fine uses the histrionic gifts of the Children of the Chapel and of Paul's.

[1] In *The Complete Works of John Lyly*, vol. ii, pp. 29 69.

VII
THOMAS KYD AND THE REVENGE TRAGEDIES

WHILE Lyly, with the help of the Children, was setting English comedy on a new road, a group of his contemporaries were rendering a parallel service to tragedy and tragi-comedy through the medium of the adult companies performing on the boards of the newly erected public theatres. It does not come within the scope of this *Introduction* to trace the history of the Elizabethan stage or the fortunes of the professional companies. Only a few facts may be briefly recalled.

In May 1574 the then all-powerful Earl of Leicester obtained for his 'servants' a royal patent, allowing them to perform within the City and liberties of London and any other city, borough, or town. The Common Council, however, laid a ban upon the performance of plays within the City jurisdiction. Thereupon James Burbage, the leader of Leicester's Company, made a counter-move in 1576 by building the first public playhouse, the *Theater*, in the liberty of Holywell in Shoreditch, outside the City boundaries. Shortly afterwards another playhouse, the *Curtain*, was built close by. But after some years the centre of theatrical activity shifted from Shoreditch to the south of the river. The *Rose* under the management of Philip Henslowe was built on the Bankside about 1587, and was followed by the *Swan* in 1594. At the end of 1598 Cuthbert and Richard Burbage, the sons of James, having quarrelled with their landlord about the renewal of the lease of the *Theater*, pulled down the building and used the timber for the construction of the *Globe*, the famous 'wooden O' on the Bankside. James Burbage in 1596 purchased property from Sir William More for the purpose of establishing a second *Blackfriars* theatre, but could not carry out his plans before his death in 1597. In 1600 Richard leased the premises to Henry Evans for performances by the Children of the Chapel, which, though 'under the name of a private house', were practically public. In the same year Philip Henslowe and his son-in-law Edward Alleyn opened up a new theatrical district by building the *Fortune* (the contract of which is still preserved at Dulwich), just outside Cripplegate, near the north-west boundary of the City, and not within the jurisdiction of the Lord Mayor.[1]

It was one or other of these theatres that were the more or less permanent homes of the great professional companies that were to make the last quarter of a century of Elizabeth's reign a glorious epoch in the history of the stage. But the companies often acted at 'command' performances in the royal palaces, and they went on long provincial tours. The most notable are Lord Leicester's, Lord Strange's, the Earl of Pembroke's, the Queen's, the Lord Chamberlain's, and the Lord Admiral's. There were transferences of actors from one company to another, and one specially notable amalgamation of Lord Strange's and the Admiral's men from about 1590 to 1594. From the latter year to the end of Elizabeth's reign the Lord Chamberlain's, headed by Richard Burbage, and including William Kempe, William Slye, and Shakespeare, and the Lord Admiral's, headed by Edward Alleyn and financed by Henslowe, were the two leading

[1] Further details on Elizabethan theatres and on the methods of performance in them may be found in two of the 'World's Manuals', *Shakespeare, the Man and his Stage*, pp. 76–104, and *An Introduction to the Reading of Shakespeare*, pp. 26–36.

companies. It was a period made illustrious by what has been very rare in our theatrical annals, the simultaneous appearance of actors and dramatists of genius.

Recent investigation indicates that among the playwrights whose work gained wide popularity on the boards of the popular theatres in the eighties of the sixteenth century the earliest was Thomas Kyd. Born in November 1558, he was the son of Francis Kyd, a London citizen and a scrivener or law-stationer, who in 1580 became a warden of the Scriveners' Company. Thomas was sent in October 1565 to the newly founded Merchant Taylors' School, where one of his contemporaries was Edmund Spenser. Under the head mastership of Richard Mulcaster who, as another pupil relates, 'yeerly . . . presented sum playes to the court, in which his scholers wear only actors . . . and by that meanes taughte them good behaviour and audacitye', Kyd became familiar from an early age with plays and playing. And if, as there is reason to think, he did not proceed to the University but followed for a time his father's occupation, it was at Merchant Taylors' that he chiefly acquired that knowledge of Latin literature, and of Senecan tragedy in particular, that he was to turn to such account on the public stage.

We have seen above how the lawyers of Inns of Court had written tragedies on the model of the Roman philosopher-dramatist. They had diverged in certain important respects from that model, but they had preserved its essential spirit, which subordinated action and character-drawing to rhetoric and moralizing. It was Kyd who took the lead in a movement that transferred to the boards of the new public theatres much of the machinery and something of the rhetoric of Senecan tragedy, but made them serve the purposes of an exciting plot and a strongly featured set of stage figures. Our knowledge of Kyd's part in this movement is curiously indirect. Ben Jonson in his lines prefixed to the first folio of Shakespeare's plays puns upon his name as 'sporting Kyd', but merely tells us that Shakespeare outshone him. Fortunately Thomas Heywood in his pamphlet *The Apology for Actors* (1612) mentions Kyd as the author of *The Spanish Tragedy*, from which he quotes a few lines. Yet not one of the ten extant editions of the play, from about 1592 to 1633, gives his name on the title-page or that of the company which performed the play. Moreover the earliest and best of these editions, though a very faulty 'first impression' has disappeared, is undated.

But there are allusions that make it probable that Kyd was writing for the stage by 1585 and *The Spanish Tragedy* may well go back to that year or a little later. If so, Kyd seems to have just preceded Marlowe in making blank verse the instrument of tragedy on the public stage. But his success was not due, like that of Marlowe, to poetic genius. He owed it to what we now call his 'sense of the theatre' and his technical skill in plot-construction. He found or invented (for no source for it has as yet been discovered) a story which illustrated after a novel fashion the traditional Senecan 'revenge' motive, and which exploited for a popular audience the devices of the Ghost and the Chorus.

The central figure of the play is Hieronimo, the Knight-Marshal of Spain. His son Horatio loves and is loved by Belimperia, a high-born lady, formerly betrothed to Don Andrea, who was slain in battle by the Portuguese Prince, Balthasar. The Prince, while a captive in the Spanish Court, becomes enamoured of Belimperia, and his suit is favoured by her ambitious and crafty brother Lorenzo, who contrives the murder of Horatio while he and Belimperia are secretly meeting at night. Belimperia's cries for help rouse Hieronimo, who comes forth 'in his shirt' with words that were to echo for years through the Elizabethan theatres (II. v):

> What out-cries pluck me from my naked bed,
> And chill my throbbing heart with trembling fear,
> Which never danger yet could daunt before?
> Who calls Hieronimo? Speak, here I am.
>
> . . . .
>
> But stay, what murderous spectacle is this?
> A man hanged up and all the murderers gone.
> And in my bower, to lay the guilt on me.
> This place was made for pleasure not for death.
> These garments that he wears I oft have seen.
> Alas, it is Horatio, my sweet son!
> O no, but he that whilome was my son.

Henceforth his one aim is to take revenge on his son's murderers. But he deliberates and dallies, unpacks his heart in paradoxical outbursts (III. ii):

> O eyes, no eyes, but fountains fraught with tears!
> O life, no life, but lively form of death!
> O world, no world, but mass of public wrongs,
> Confused and filled with murder and misdeeds!

and becomes at times distraught. But he regains his self-control and executes his long-delayed purpose by means of a stratagem. He arranges for a dramatic version of the story of Soliman and Perseda to be performed by himself and the other chief personages. In this 'play within the play', while the spectators think that they are watching a mere make-believe he kills Balthasar, and Belimperia stabs Lorenzo to death, both afterwards committing suicide. But even this holocaust

The Spanish Tragedie:
OR,
Hieronimo is mad againe.

Containing the lamentable end of *Don Horatio*, and *Belimperia*; with the pittifull death of *Hieronimo*.

Newly corrected, amended, and enlarged with new Additions of the *Painters* part, and others, as it hath of late been diuers times acted.

LONDON,
Printed by W. White, for I. White and T. Langley, and are to be sold at their Shop ouer against the Sarazens head without New-gate. 1615

Title-page of the 1615 quarto edition of *The Spanish Tragedy*, with a woodcut illustrating the scene of Horatio's murder.
From a copy in the British Museum Library.

does not fully satisfy the Ghost of Andrea and Revenge, who have acted as Chorus throughout, and Revenge sinks out of sight with the words:

> Then haste we down to meet thy friends and foes:
> To place thy friends in ease, the rest in woes.
> For here though death hath end their misery,
> I'll there begin their endless tragedy.

The accumulation of horrors at the close of the play has earned for Kyd in many of the text-books the reputation of a 'blood and thunder' dramatist. And it is true that there are cruder features in his flamboyant art that appealed to the far from sensitive theatrical audiences of his day. Moreover he had a flair for catch-phrases (some of them quoted above), e.g. Hieronimo's 'naked bed', 'eyes no eyes', 'go by, Jeronimo', which were over and over again repeated and parodied by his contemporaries. But his real dramatic genius lay in what would to-day be called his gift of psycho-analysis, shown in his delineation of Hieronimo, and his skill in the management of plot. The best way to realize this skill is to see a performance of the play as recently given by academic amateurs at Oxford and in London. In the editions of *The Spanish Tragedy* from 1602 onwards there are some remarkable 'additions', including a dialogue between Hieronimo at midnight in his garden with a painter, whom he asks, 'can'st paint me a tear, or a wound, a groan or a sigh?' This episode is a masterpiece of romantic writing, as was recognized by Charles Lamb, but it and the other additions, when the play is performed, are found to hamper the action, and interfere with Kyd's ingenious design.

Henslowe records in his *Diary* that on 25 September 1601 and 22 June 1602 he made payments to Ben Jonson for additions to the play. But it is doubtful if these were ever printed, for nothing could be more unlike Jonson's style, with its mingling of realism and classicism, than the additions in the 1602 quarto. Henslowe also recorded some performances in the first half of 1592 of a play that he calls *Don Horatio* or *The Comedy of Jeronimo*, which seems to have been a fore-piece to *The Spanish Tragedy*. If this was from the hand of Kyd, it is not to be identified with the extant burlesque piece *The First Part of Jeronimo*, which was published in 1605, and which on internal evidence was probably written about that time.

There is much more reason for ascribing to him the anonymous *Soliman and Perseda* of which the earliest edition is undated, but which was entered on the Stationers' Register in November 1592. It deals with the same subject as Hieronimo's play in *The Spanish Tragedy*, and in plot-construction and style it is akin to Kyd's work. It gives more prominence, however, to a comic underplot, which contains the figure of Basilisco, a braggart soldier, whom Shakespeare remembered when he wrote *King John*, I. i. 243–4. If the play is not by Kyd himself, it belongs, to use the language of the art galleries, to his 'school'. But there is an even more interesting problem in connexion with a lost *Hamlet* play which preceded Shakespeare's great tragedy. When Robert Greene's novel *Menaphon* was published in 1589 there was prefixed to it an Epistle by Thomas Nashe which contains the following passage:

> It is a common practise now a daies amongst a sort of shifting companions, that runne through euery art and thriue by none to leaue the trade of *Nouerint*, whereto they were borne, and busie themselues with the indeuours of art, that could scarcelie latinise their neck-verse if they should haue neede; yet English Seneca read by candle-light

> yeeldes manie good sentences as '*bloud is a begger*' and so forth: and if you intreate him faire in a frostie morning, he will affoord you whole *Hamlets*, I should say handfulls of tragical speeches. But o griefe! *tempus edax rerum*; what's that will last alwaies? The sea exhaled by droppes will in continuance be drie, and Seneca let bloud line by line, and page by page, at length must needes die to our stage: which makes his famisht followers to imitate the Kidde in *Aesop*, who enamoured with the Foxes newfangles, forsook all hopes of life to leape into a new occupation; and these men renowncing all possibilities of credit or estimation, to intermeddle with Italian translations.

It is evident that Nashe alludes here to a play on Hamlet in Senecan style. The reference to 'the Kidde in *Aesop*' seems to be a pun on Kyd's name, and 'the trade of *Nouerint*' (from the legal formula, *Noverint universi per praesentes*) is that of a scrivener, whereto he was born. Moreover he had intermeddled with Italian translations by producing an English version of one of Tasso's prose works. There are other details in Nashe's epistle which give support to the belief (though it is not shared by all scholars) that it was Kyd who wrote a play on Hamlet which has been lost. Some critics have thought that Shakespeare made use of it, and that phrases from it are preserved in the first, imperfect, quarto of his *Hamlet*. However this may be, *The Spanish Tragedy*, with a father's delayed revenge for a murdered son, is a remarkable counterpart to *Hamlet*, with a son's delayed revenge for a murdered father, while the Ghost and the play within the play are common to both.

It is at any rate certain that Kyd was personally acquainted with Christopher Marlowe. They both became involved in charges of 'atheism' in May 1593, and in a letter defending himself Kyd refers to an occasion when he and Marlowe were writing 'in one chamber' two years ago. Unfortunately we do not know whether they were engaged in dramatic collaboration. The only work of Kyd's published in 1594, at the close of which he died, was his translation of a neo-Senecan play *Cornélie* by the French dramatist, Garnier.

It was probably only to please a lady patron, the Countess of Sussex, that the author of *The Spanish Tragedy* spent any pains on so academic a piece of work as *Cornelia*. But two contemporary publications, *Locrine* (1595) and *The First Part of the Tragical Reign of Selimus* (1594), show that there were dramatists, writing for the popular stage, who were making use of the conventional Senecan machinery and rhetoric, combined with crude humour, but without the higher elements of Kyd's technique and psychology. *Locrine*, like *Gorboduc*, draws its plot from mythical British history, and, as in the earlier play, each Act is preceded by a symbolical dumb-show which is interpreted by Ate the Fury, as presenter. The dying King Brutus divides his Kingdom among his sons, Locrine, Camber, and Albanact. After his death Britain is invaded by the Scythians, headed by their King Humber, accompanied by his wife Estrild, and his son Hubba. They win a victory in which Albanact is slain, and Locrine, acting on the maxim,

> He loves not most that doth lament the most,
> But he that seeks to venge the injury,

vows to seek satisfaction for his brother's blood:

> For this revenge, for this sweet word, revenge,
> Must ease and cease thy wrongful injuries.

These four lines contain in them the essence of all the

'revenge' tragedies, and when Locrine marches to battle against the Scythians, the ghost of Albanact appears to Humber, shrieking 'Revenge, revenge for blood'. From one evil springs another. Locrine defeats Humber and puts him to flight, but becomes enamoured of his wife Estrild for whom he builds an underground pleasure-house, deserting his own queen and cousin, Gwendolen. After seven years, that he may enjoy his guilty love openly at the Court, he makes away with Gwendolen's father, the aged Corineus, whose Ghost in its turn cries for revenge on Locrine. This is achieved by Gwendolen, with the aid of her brother and son. Locrine and Estrild kill themselves on the field of battle, and their young daughter, Sabren, drowns herself in the 'pleasant stream' which thenceforward was to bear, in the variant spelling 'Severn', her name. And by another variant she is invoked to rise again at the close of *Comus* in one of the loveliest of Milton's lyrics:

> Sabrina fair,
> Listen where thou art sitting
> Under the glassy, cool, translucent wave.

The poet's vision of her, attended by her water-nymphs, carries us far away from the ghosts, murders, and suicides of this Senecan tragedy. There is, however, an attempt in *Locrine* to relieve the horrors by a very loosely strung comic underplot, of which the chief figure is a fantastical cobbler, Strumbo, whom we see and hear, with his lady-love Dorothy, and his man, Trompart, cobbling shoes and singing in praise of their craft:

> *Tromp.* We cobblers lead a merry life.
> *All.* Dan, dan, dan, dan.
> *Strumb.* Void of all envy and of strife.
> *All.* Dan, diddle, dan.

Whatever the publisher may have meant by stating on

the title-page of the 1595 quarto that the play was 'Newly set foorth, overseene and corrected, By W. S.', the editors of the Third Folio were very uncritical in including it among Shakespeare's work. Whoever the author was, he borrowed lines and phrases freely from Spenser's *Complaints* (1590), and the play contains many echoes from contemporary pieces.

These borrowings from Spenser, to which are added some from *The Faerie Queene*, are found also in *Selimus*, which further reproduces many lines from *Locrine*. The two plays are thus linked, but otherwise they present striking contrasts. The larger part of *Selimus* is not in blank verse, but in rhyme, including numerous stanzaic passages. It has no Chorus, Dumb Show, or Ghost. Its subject is taken not from a legendary British era, but from recent Turkish history. Its central figure is the grandfather of the reigning Sultan. Though the 'revenge' theme enters into it, the play throws into high relief another of the chief features of Senecan tragedy, the tyrant. As the prologue states, it presents in Selimus 'the image of an implacable king'. He wades to the Turkish throne through blood, poisoning his father, and strangling his elder brothers and all others who stand in his path. Only in the later scenes is there some slight attempt at comic relief, and the audiences, when the Queen's Company (as we learn from the title-page) acted the play, must have had strong stomachs. But there are some interesting reflective passages, as when Selimus describes a primitive golden age before there was need of kings, laws, or religion:

> When first this circled round, this building fair,
> Some God took out of the confused mass,
> (What God I do not know, nor greatly care)
>
> . . . .

War was not then, and riches were not known,
And no man said, 'this, or this, is mine own'.
The plough-man with a furrow did not mark
How far his great possessions did reach:
The earth knew not the share, nor seas the bark,
The soldiers entered not the battered breach
Nor trumpets the tantara loud did teach.
There needed then no judge, nor yet no law,
Nor any king of whom to stand in awe.

These revenge tragedies made a strong appeal to the excitable emotions of the Elizabethan groundlings, but the extravagance of their passions and language, often ill-matched with crude stage-devices and equipment, provoked a reaction to more homely criminal themes and more realistic treatment. In the 'Induction' to *A Warning for Fair Women*, an anonymous play published in 1599, History, Tragedy, and Comedy have a dispute. Tragedy bids the other two quit the stage, and cries,

I must have passions that must move the soul;
Make the heart heavy and throb within the bosom,
Extorting tears out of the strictest eyes . . .
This is my office:

whereupon Comedy retorts:

How some damn'd tyrant to obtain a crown
Stabs, hangs, imprisons, smothers, cutteth throats;
And then a Chorus too, comes howling in
And tells us of the worrying of a cat:
Then too, a filthy whining ghost,
Lapt in some foul sheet, or a leather pilch
Comes screaming like a pig half stick'd,
And cries *Vindicta!*—Revenge!—Revenge!
With that a little rosin flasheth forth,
Like smoke out of a tobacco pipe, or a boy's squib.

Tragedy's answer is to whip her rivals off, and then she appeals to the spectators:

Give entertainment unto Tragedy.
My scene is London, native and your own.
I sigh to think my subject too well known,
I am not feigned.

These words, with variant place-names instead of London, would serve to introduce the remarkable group of plays based on recent murders, of which the earliest is *Arden of Feversham* (1592). Here too the author in the closing lines contrasts with artificial inventions

this naked tragedy,
Wherein no filed points are foisted in
To make it gracious to the ear or eye;
For simple truth is gracious enough,
And needs no other points of glosing stuff.

But though he does not use 'glosing stuff' he has a sure and fine dramatic instinct that elevates a 'Newgate Calendar' crime into a deeply moving work of art. This narrative of the murder of Thomas Ardern (as the name was actually spelt) of Faversham in Kent, in February 1551, was found by the playwright in Holinshed's *Chronicle*. He individualized all the personages in this dark crime of the Kentish countryside—Arden, the weak, uxurious husband; Mosbie, the low-born but fascinating steward in a great house who steals the affections of Arden's wife, Alice; the villainous agents, Michael and Greene, Shakebag and Black Will, and, above all, Alice Arden herself, the *bourgeoise* Clytemnestra, as she has been called, who dares everything to satisfy her guilty passion:

Sweet Mosbie is the man that hath my heart
. . . .
Love is a god, and marriage is but words:
And therefore Mosbie's title is the best.
Tush! whether it be or no, he shall be mine,
In spite of him, of Hymen, and of rites.

Fortune seeks to save her from herself by baffling, one after another, her and Mosbie's plans for doing away with Arden. But she never falters in her pitiless determination till he is trapped during a game of tables (backgammon) in his own house. When the others have dealt their blows, and he lies groaning, she finishes the deed of blood:

> nay, then give me the weapon!
> Take this for hindering Mosbie's love and mine!

When Arden's body has been carried into the counting-house, she cries, 'fetch water and wash away this blood'. The words anticipate those of Lady Macbeth's after Duncan's murder, 'A little water clears us of this deed'. But Swinburne went astray in claiming *Arden* for Shakespeare, who never handled these lurid contemporary episodes. A more plausible case has been made out for Kyd, but the play is probably from the pen of one who was influenced by the more realistic side of Kyd's work, and whom we would give more to identify than any other of the 'unknowns' of the Elizabethan theatre.

A Warning for Fair Women, from whose Induction some pungent lines have been quoted, was acted by the Lord Chamberlain's Company. As with *Arden* its subject is a notorious recent crime, 'the most Tragicall and Lamentable Murther of Master George Sanders of London', in 1573, by George Browne, with the consent of his wife, and with Mistress Drury and her man, 'Trusty Roger', as accomplices. The play has a racy vigour which doubtless made it effective on the stage, but it lacks the transforming touches of *Arden*. In addition to the Induction and Epilogue there are elaborate Dumb-Shows in which allegorical figures mingle with the chief characters. The murky rhetoric in which

Tragedy expounds the meaning of these 'Shows' is in uneasy contrast with the homely dialogue of the main action which follows with pedantic closeness the details of the pamphlet which was the dramatist's source. Hence after Browne has murdered Sanders, of whose wife he has become enamoured, a disproportionate number of scenes are occupied with the judicial proceedings which brought the various culprits to their doom. Browne's execution appears to have been presented on the stage, for after his last speech and confession, according to the stage-direction, 'he leapes off'. There is realism of an absurdly different type in the last interview between Mistress Anne Sanders and her children when she presents each of them with a copy of Bradford's *Godly Meditations*:[1]

> Sleep not without them, when you go to bed,
> And rise a mornings with them in your hands.

A playwright who had shown no little skill in the characterization of Anne herself, of Browne who seeks to the end to save her, and of the unscrupulous go-between, Nan Drury, ought to have known better than to follow his source to such an anti-climax. But the truth is he had divided aims as a dramatist and a moralist, and he meant the 'warning' in his title to be taken seriously, as happened with a play of which he tells an edifying tale:

> A woman that had made away her husband,
> And sitting to behold a tragedy
> At Linn, a town in Norfolk,
> Acted by players travelling that way—
> Wherein a woman that had murthered hers
> Was ever haunted by her husband's ghost,
> The passion written by a feeling pen,

[1] An edifying treatise by John Bradford, first published in 1597.

And acted by a good tragedian—
She was so moved by the sight thereof,
As she cried out, the play was made by[1] her,
And openly confessed her husband's murder.

It was probably the same story that Shakespeare had in mind in Hamlet's words:

I have heard
That guilty creatures sitting at a play
Have by the very cunning of the scene
Been struck so to the soul that presently[2]
They have proclaim'd their malefactions.

When the Prince of Denmark had the murder of Gonzago enacted before King Claudius he was borrowing for use in the highest court circles an instrument for 'unkennelling' guilt which domestic tragedy had exploited in a humbler sphere.

[1] 'By' here = 'about'.

[2] immediately.

VIII

CHRONICLE-HISTORY AND BIOGRAPHICAL PLAYS

In the Induction to *A Warning for Fair Women*, History, as has been seen, appeared with Tragedy and Comedy, and had made her exit with the cry:

> And, Tragedy, although to-day thou reign,
> To-morrow here I'll domineer again.

By 1599 such a boast could be fairly made, but it was not till the closing decade of the sixteenth century that the chronicle-history play had fully established its place in the public theatre. Yet in a hybrid form, in John Bale's *King Johan*, it had made one memorable contribution to English drama during the reign of Henry VIII. Bale was a contemporary of the group of early Tudor playwrights discussed in the first chapter of this book, and he had gifts which might have given him a prominent place among them. But his violent Protestantism led him to subordinate his ambitions as a dramatist to bitter religious propaganda.

Bale was born near Dunwich in Suffolk in 1495. His early training was under the Carmelites. He took orders, but in the early 'thirties of the sixteenth century or perhaps before, was converted to Lutheranism. Thomas Cromwell gave him his protection, but when he fell from power in 1540, Bale had to vacate the vicarage of Thorndon and flee to Germany. After the accession of Edward VI he returned, and in 1553 became Bishop of Ossory in Ireland. During Mary's reign he had a second period of exile at Basle. Under

Elizabeth he again returned and remained at Canterbury till his death in 1563.

A list drawn up by himself in 1536 includes the titles of fourteen comedies or tragedies in English from his pen. A later list in 1548 extends the number to twenty-two. They are on Scriptural or controversial religious themes. Four of them, assigned to 1538, have come down in printed form. Of these *God's Promises*, *John Baptist*, and *The Temptation of Christ* are belated *Miracle* plays, while *Three Laws* (those of Nature, Moses, and Christ) introduces allegorical figures after the manner of a *Morality*. All, especially *Three Laws*, are strongly Protestant in tone. At first sight *King Johan* might seem to stand apart, but in spite of its title, it is a strange 'contamination' of a *Morality* and a history play, and in essence it is not a drama but a fiercely polemical tract. It has been preserved in a manuscript which passed from the Corporation of Ipswich to the Duke of Devonshire, at Chatsworth, and thence to the Huntington Library in California. Though an edition was printed from the manuscript in 1838, this was in various ways defective, and it is only quite recently that in one of the Malone Society's reprints a full and completely documented text has been provided.

Here it is enough to say that Bale is the sole author of the play, but that the manuscript is in two hands, one that of a scribe, the other that of Bale who revised and added to the original text. As *King Johan* is included in his 1536 list, it must have been written before then in its earliest form, which was in two 'Books' or 'Parts'. It was almost certainly the play performed by 'Bale and his ffelowes' before the Archbishop of Canterbury on 2 January 1539 which showed King John to be 'as noble a prince as ever was in England'.

Englande. If ye love me syr, for Gods sake do never so

K. Johan. O Englande, Englande, shewe now thyselfe a mother
Thy people wyll els, be slayne here without nomber
As God shall iudge me, I do not thys of cowardnesse
But of compassyon, in thys extreme heavynesse
Shall my people shedde, their bloude in suche habundance
Naye, I shall rather, gyve up my whole governance

Sedicyon. Come of apace than, and make an ende of it shortly

Englande. The most pytiefull chaunce, yt hath bene hytherto surely

K. Johan. Here I submytt me, etc.

Englande. So noble a realme, to stande tributarye alas
To the devyls vycar, suche fortune never was

Sedicyon. Out with thys harlot, cockes soule she hath lete a fart

Englande. Lyke a wretche thu hest, thy report is lyke as thu art
ye shall suffer the monkes etc.

A portion of fol. 23 b (page 40) of *King Johan*
in Bishop Bale's handwriting
From the manuscript in the Henry E. Huntington Library, San Marino, California

There is evidence that suggests that the version then acted was a one-part play and corresponds with the scribe's portion of the extant manuscript, and that the additions in Bale's writing represent a double revision in the reigns of Edward VI and Elizabeth. It is certainly Elizabeth to whom the closing lines refer, beginning:

> Englande hath a quene, Thankes to the lorde aboue
> whych maye be a lyghte, to other princes all
> for the godly wayes, whome she doth dayly moue
> To hir liege people, through Gods wurde specyall.

The lines would be appropriate if the play was acted before the Queen on her visit to Ipswich in August 1561, to which the preservation of the manuscript there gives plausibility. In any case in its final form it was again a two-part piece, with an 'Interpreter' appearing in the interval. The *dramatis personae* are puzzling, for not only is there a mingling of historical and allegorical characters, but in some cases they are identified, while in others the parts are merely doubled. Thus Sedition changes his dress into that of Civil Order and back again, and afterwards becomes identified with Steven Langton. Other identifications, certain or probable, are Dissimulation and Simon of Swynsett, Private Wealth and Cardinal Pandulphus, Usurped Power and the Pope. On the other hand, England, a widow, merely doubles parts with the Clergy. Amidst these complications one figure stands out in bold relief, that of King John. To those who think of him as the extortioner, compelled to sign the Great Charter at Runnymede, or as the Shakespearian half-hearted criminal, it is difficult to accept him as here presented, in the light of a national hero. But as two centuries later Thomas Gray could overlook everything in the career of Henry VIII except that he was

> the majestic lord
> That broke the bonds of Rome,

so in Henry's own reign Bale could only see in John the protagonist in an earlier struggle with the Papacy, till he was overborne by the banded powers of evil. As the Interpreter sets it forth:

> Vpon a good zele, he attempted very farre
> For welthe of this realme to prouyde reformacyon
> In the churche thereof, but they ded him debarre
> Of that good purpose, for by excommunycacyon
> The space of vij. yeares, they interdyct thy[s] nacyon,
> These bloodsuppers thus, of crueltie and spyght
> Subdued thys good kynge for executynge right.
>
> . . . .
>
> Thys noble kynge Iohan, as a faythfull Moyses
> Withstoode proude Pharao, for hys poore Israel
> Myndynge to brynge it, out of the lande of Darkenesse
> But the Egyptyanes did agaynst hym so rebell
> That hys poore people ded styll in the desart dwell
> Tyll that duke Iosue, whych was our late Kyng Henrye
> Clerely brought vs in, to the lande of mylke and honye.

John had been the Moses, Henry had been the Joshua of the conflict. Elizabeth in the closing lines of the play is hailed as the Daniel:

> In Danyels sprete, she hath subdued the Papistes
> With all the ofsprynge, of Antichristes generacyon.

Had Bale lived later than 1563, it is doubtful if he would have been satisfied with Elizabeth's somewhat Laodicean religious policy. And he would not have approved of the picture of his Protestant hero in *The Troublesome Raigne of King John*, acted by the Queen's Company and published in 1591. For in this anonymous two-part play the interest in the first Part is mainly concentrated in the King's designs against his nephew Arthur, the rival claimant to the throne, whose cause has a passionate advocate in his mother, Constance, and a champion in Philip of France, till he is bought off by a marriage between the Dauphin and John's niece, the Lady Blanche. And who could recognize Bale's patriotic king in the John who orders Hubert de Burgh to put out Arthur's eyes and drives his subjects to rebellion? As he himself laments,

> Now they shun me as a serpent's sting,
> A tragic tyrant, stern and pitiless;
> And not a title follows after John
> But butcher, blood-sucker, and murderer.

In the role of English champion the playwright substitutes for John, the fictitious but highly effective figure of Philip Fauconbridge, a bastard son of the great Richard of the lion heart. There is one moment when John takes courage to defy Pandulph, the Papal Legate:

> Know, sir priest, as I honour the Church and holy churchmen, so I scorn to be subject to the greatest prelate in the world. Tell thy master so from me, and say John of England said it, that never an Italian priest of them all shall either have tithe, toll, or polling-penny out of England; but as I am king, so will I reign next under God, supreme head both over spiritual and temporal.

But when Pandulph excommunicates him, and the nobles in the second Part of the play join with the invading Dauphin to depose him, he eats all his brave words, and surrenders his crown to the Legate. But this submission comes too late, and he has to fly before his enemies, and seek refuge in Swinstead Abbey, whose treasures he had despoiled, and where he is poisoned by a monk in revenge. And with his last breath, like the Interpreter in Bale's play, he predicts to Fauconbridge the advent of Henry VIII:

> My tongue doth falter: Philip, I tell thee, man,
> Since John did yield unto the priest of Rome,
> Nor he nor his have prosp'red on the earth:
> Curst are his blessings, and his curse is bliss.
>
> . . . . . .
>
> But if my dying heart deceive me not,
> From out these loins shall spring a kingly brand
> Whose arms shall reach unto the gates of Rome,
> And with his feet tread down the strumpet's pride
> That sits upon the chair of Babylon.

Such lines would win ready applause from an Elizabethan audience, which would also find a topical significance in the Bastard's closing words:

> If England's peers and people join in one,
> Nor Pope, nor France, nor Spain can do them wrong.

The Troublesome Raigne, though loosely constructed, is a vigorous piece of work and well deserved to be taken by Shakespeare as the immediate model of his own *King John*.

Another play which furnished material to Shakespeare is *The Famous Victories of Henry the Fifth*, published in 1598, but dating from before the death in 1588 of Tarlton, who acted in it. The piece ranges superficially over the ground covered by the two Parts of *King Henry IV* and *King Henry V*, for it begins with an episode in which Prince Henry takes part with two boon companions, Ned and Tom, in robbing his father's officers, and it ends with his betrothal to Princess Katherine of France. Sir John Oldcastle is mentioned as taking part in the robbery, though he only makes a brief appearance later, and does not appear in person in the Eastcheap Tavern scene which ends with an incident told to a group of gaping tradesmen by the Vintner's boy:

> Why this night about two hours ago, there came the young Prince, and three or four more of his companions, and called for wine good store, and then they sent for a noise[1] of musicians and were very merry for the space of an hour; then whether their music liked them not, or whether they had drunk too much wine or no, I cannot tell, but our pots flew against the walls, and then they drew their swords and went into the street and fought, and some took one part, and some took another, but for the space of half an hour, there was such a bloody fray as passeth, and none could part them until such time as the Mayor and Sheriff were sent for, and then at the last with much ado they took them, and so the young Prince was carried to the Counter.[2]

Though this episode does not appear in *King Henry IV*, the general spirit of the Eastcheap scenes, and of the madcap Prince's frolics, is here vividly anticipated. But it is in the serious scenes, especially the interviews between the Prince and his father, that *The Famous Victories* foreshadows still more clearly situations and parts of the dialogue in the Shakespearian plays. Thus after Prince Henry's explanation that he took the crown away from his father's bedchamber, because he thought that he was already dead, the King cries:

> God give thee joy, my son,
> God bless thee and make thee his servant,
> And send thee a prosperous reign;
> For God knows, my son, how hardly I came by it,
> And how hardly I have maintained it.

[1] Band. [2] A London prison.

And the Prince answers:

Howsoever you came by it, I know not,
But now I have it from you, and from you I will keep it:
And he that seeks to take the crown from my head
Let him look that his armour be thicker than mine.

Shakespeare must have had these lines before him when he wrote:

King Henry IV. God knows, my son,
By what by-paths and indirect crook'd ways
I met this crown; and I myself know well
How troublesome it sat upon my head;
To thee it shall descend with better quiet,
Better opinion, better confirmation.
. . . .
Prince Henry. My gracious liege,
You won it, wore it, kept it, gave it me;
Then plain and right must my possession be;
Which I, with more than with a common pain,
'Gainst all the world will rightfully maintain.

The anonymous playwright is less successful with 'the famous victories', crowned by 'the honourable battle of Agincourt' which give the piece its title, but in the 'plain terms' wooing of Princess Kate he again set the fashion for his great successor.

In *King Leir and his three Daughters*, published in 1605 but entered in the Stationers' Register in 1594, a French king woos a British princess, Cordella, and his army is victorious on British soil. Here the playwright subordinated patriotism to what he deemed to be historical truth as he found it in Holinshed's *Chronicle*. For to the Tudor mind these legends of early Britain had as authentic warrant as the records of Plantagenet days. And the anonymous author of *King Leir* (he adopts Holinshed's spelling of the name) fashioned out of the story of the old king and his three daughters, not a Senecan tragedy like *Gorboduc*, but a chronicle-history of varied interest. Many of the features of the Shakespearian *King Lear* are absent: the Fool, the storm, and the king's madness; the whole of the Gloucester underplot, with the bastard Edmund and the feigned Tom o' Bedlam, Edgar; the deaths of Lear and Cordelia and the majestic sweep of the entire action that makes of *King Lear* a tragedy on epic scale. It was only perversity that could lead Tolstoy to set the older play above the Shakespearian masterpiece. But on the other hand we must not through our familiarity with *King Lear* underrate the merits of the anonymous play. It creates Perillus, the faithful and clear-sighted follower of the King, who was a model for Shakespeare's Kent. It makes much of the love of the King of Gallia for Cordella, which yet cannot displace her love for the father who has used her so ill:

> Yet pardon me, my gracious Lord, in this:
> For what can stop the course of nature's powers?
> As easy is it for four-footed beasts
> To stay themselves upon the liquid air,
> And mount aloft into the element,
> And overstrip the feathered fowls in flight:
> As easy is it for the finny fish
> To live and thrive without the help of water:
> As easy is it for the Blackamoor
> To wash the tawny colour from his skin,
> Which all oppose against the course of nature,
> As I am able to forget my father.

Leir, when his elder daughters have turned him adrift and sought to have him murdered, cannot believe that

Cordella will give him welcome. In Euphuistic phrases he cries:

> Can kindness spring out of ingratitude?
> Or love be reaped, where hatred hath been sown?
> Can henbane join in league with mithridate?
> Or sugar grow in wormwoods bitter stalk?
> It cannot be, they are too opposite.

But Perillus reassures him:

> Fear not, my lord, the perfect good indeed
> Can never be corrupted by the bad.
>
> . . . .
>
> And therefore, though you name yourself the thorn,
> The weed, the gall, the henbane and the wormwood,
> Yet she'll continue in her former state,
> The hony, milk, grape, sugar, mithridate.

So it proves, and, as in the original story, with the help of Cordella and her husband, Leir is restored to the throne of Britain, and his wrongs avenged.

It is curious that while primitive British annals provided Elizabethan drama with such fruitful themes, the illustrious Anglo-Saxon line was almost entirely neglected. An interesting chronicle-history, *Edmond Ironside*, forms one of the collection of manuscript plays in the British Museum, Egerton 1994. Nearly all these plays belong to the Stuart period, and we cannot therefore be certain that *Edmond Ironside* is of earlier origin, though its metrical characteristics would suggest that it dates from the last decade of the sixteenth century. However this may be, the play presents a vigorously drawn portrait of Edmund Ironside, an English patriot king, contrasted with his Danish rival, Canute. Between them stands the crafty Earl Edric, a Machiavellian intriguer, who sides with each in turn, and whose self-interested plots are foiled when at the close the two kings seal a contract of amity.

To the same Egerton 1994 collection belongs a play dealing with episodes that cover the greater part of Richard II's reign. It has no title in the manuscript, but is now generally known as *Thomas of Woodstock*, the family name of the Duke of Gloucester, the King's uncle, who is the chief character in the play. He is a patriot statesman who seeks to deliver the young King from the toils of the unscrupulous favourites, Bushy, Bagot, and Greene, and who pays the penalty of death by violence. In some grimly humorous prose scenes the reign of terror in the countryside created by Richard's 'black charters' is vividly illustrated, and the play may be read as an effective forepiece to Shakespeare's *Richard II*, which deals only with the closing period of his ill-starred career. But whether *Thomas of Woodstock* was actually written before Shakespeare's play, and was known to him, there is not sufficient evidence to show. In any case it belongs to the group of chronicle-histories in which the central figure is not a king but some other personage of high estate.

To the same group belongs *Thomas Lord Cromwell*, acted by the Lord Chamberlain's company and 'written', according to the title-page of the 1602 edition, 'by W. S.' Hence it was ascribed to Shakespeare in the Third and Fourth Folios, though perhaps no piece in the 'apocrypha' can have less claim to such an honour. In a loosely strung series of scenes based upon a section of Foxe's *Actes and Monuments* it sets forth the fortunes of Thomas Cromwell from his schooldays to his tragic end. The scene shifts abruptly from England to Antwerp, to Florence and to Mantua, and then back to England, where Cromwell's rise begins in the service of the Master of the Rolls. The two threads that knit the later scenes into a semblance of unity are his display of gratitude to his earlier benefactors and his Protestant zeal that brings him into conflict with Gardiner, Bishop of Winchester, over the dissolution of the monasteries:

Cromwell. I am no enemy to religion,
But what is done, it is for England's good.
What did they serve for but to feed a sort
Of lazy Abbots, and of full-fed Friars?
They neither plough, nor sow, and yet they reap
The fat of all the land and suck the poor.
Gardiner. God doth know the infant yet unborn
Will curse the time the Abbeys were pulled down.
I pray now where is hospitality,
Where now may poor distressed people go
For to relieve their need, or rest their bones
When weary travail doth oppress their limbs?

With the help of the great Catholic nobles Gardiner contrives his downfall, but there is no dramatic heightening of the bare historic facts.

Another of Henry VIII's ministers fills the title-part in the British Museum manuscript play, *Sir Thomas More*. Apart from the special circumstances mentioned below which have given this play exceptional interest for Elizabethan students, it has genuine dramatic merits, though these do not include unity of design. It consists of seventeen scenes which fall into three groups. The first of these (scenes i and iii–vii) deals with the anti-alien riots of the 'ill May-day' of 1517, which are quelled by the oratory of More, who is rewarded by a Knighthood and other marks of royal favour. The second group (scenes ii, viii, ix) presents various incidents from More's career while he was Sheriff, including the performance of an interlude in his house before the

Lord Mayor and Mayoress. The third group (scenes x–xvii) shows More refusing to sign certain Articles presented to him in the king's name, with his consequent fall from power, followed by his arrest, imprisonment in the Tower, and execution.

The manuscript contains the hands of no less than six contributors, three of whom have been identified by comparison with their otherwise known scripts. The writer of the original text is now known to be Anthony Munday, of whom some further account is given later in this chapter. Certain passages in this text were cancelled and replaced by insertions from the hands of other playwrights. One of these was Henry Chettle and another was Thomas Dekker. Two others are conjectural, but the hand responsible for the addition on folios 8^a, 8^b, and 9^a of the manuscript has been identified by some eminent palaeographers, after comparison with his known signatures, as that of Shakespeare. Further support for this view has been sought in parallels of spelling, phrasing, and ideas with those of Shakespeare. Thus his emphasis in *Troilus and Cressida* and in *Coriolanus* on the chaos that would result without 'degree' or authority in the state is found to be echoed in the words of More in scene vi as he pictures to the rioters the results of a successful rising against the foreigners:

graunt them remoued and graunt that this your noyce
hath Chidd downe all the maiestie of Ingland,

. . . .

what had you gott, Ile tell you, you had taught
how insolenc and strong hand shoold prevayle
how ordere shoold be quelld, and by this patterne
not on of you shoold lyve an aged man
for other ruffians as their fancies wrought

> with sealf same hand sealf reasons and sealf right
> woold shark on you and men lyke revenous fishes
> woold feed on on another.

I am not among those who confidently support Shakespeare's claim to the 'addition', but the converging lines of evidence are in its favour.

In any case the whole passage was probably never spoken on the stage, for when the manuscript was submitted to Edmund Tilney, Master of the Revels, for his licence, he wrote on the margin of the first page the stern order:

> Leaue out ye insurrection wholy & ye cause theroff & begin w^{t} Sr Tho: More att ye mayors sessions w^{t} a reportt afterwards off his good seruic don being Shriue of London vppon a mutiny agaynst ye Lumbards. Only by a shortt reportt & nott otherwise att your own perrilles.

An anti-alien riot was not a subject that Elizabeth's government wanted to have presented in a public theatre.

The episode, in Munday's hand, in the second group of scenes, of More entertaining the Lord Mayor with a play, is notable for several reasons. The players, who are supposed to be Cardinal Wolsey's servants, offer a choice of seven titles, mostly *Moralities*, but including Heywood's *The Four PP*. More chooses the *Marriage between Wit and Wisdom* (of which there is a manuscript in the British Museum), but when the players enter their dialogue is taken almost entirely from another *Morality* in their list, *Lusty Juventus*, with the names of the characters changed. But one of the actors cast for the part of Good Counsel has been sent to the wig-maker's for 'a long beard' for Wit, and is not at hand when his cue comes. So Sir Thomas himself steps into the breach (as he used to do in Cardinal Morton's household) and takes the part so successfully that one of the actors cries, 'Do ye hear, fellows? would not my Lord make a rare player?'

It is an abrupt change from such merriment to the opening scene of the third section of the play, where More and the Bishop of Rochester decline to subscribe to Articles sent from the king. Munday had to proceed cautiously here, for the Articles were those acknowledging the royal supremacy in Church as well as in State on which Elizabeth set as much store as her father. It inevitably weakens the effect of More's downfall and tragic end that we are not shown the cause for which he suffers. But the picture of his mingled gaiety and fortitude in his home at Chelsea and in the Tower is lifelike and moving, till the last scene of all:

> Oh, is this the place?
> I promise ye, it is a goodly Scaffolde.
> In sooth I am come about a headlesse arrand,
> ffor I haue not much to say, now I am heere.
> well, let 's ascend a Gods name.
> In troth me thinkes your stayre is somewhat weake,
> I pre thee, honest friend, lend me thy hand,
> To help me vp: As for my comming downe,
> let me alone, Ile looke to that my selfe.

The recent recognition of Munday as having the chief hand in *Sir Thomas More* had added to the reputation of a writer whose versatility was hitherto his chief claim to remembrance. Born in 1553, the son of a London draper, he had been a stationer's apprentice, a spy upon the Jesuits in Rome, a Messenger of the Chamber, and an actor. He had written ballads, lyrics, and pamphlets, and had translated French and Spanish romances. In later years—he survived till

1633—he was to write pageants for the City companies. His activities as a playwright appear to have begun about 1594. His name as a joint-author of many pieces, most of which have been lost, occurs frequently in Henslowe's *Diary* between 1597 and 1602. Meres in 1598 includes him among 'the best for comedy', and strangely singles him out as 'our best plotter'. None of his extant plays justifies such a designation. *John a Kent and John a Cumber*, preserved in an autograph signed manuscript dated December 1596, is a fanciful and intricate piece in which an English wizard, John a Kent, aids two noble ladies to be united to their true loves while his Scottish rival, John a Cumber, employs his arts, for a time successfully, on behalf of the suitors favoured by their family. Turnop and 'his crew of clowns' who present 'a country merriment' to these suitors have a touch of kinship with Bottom and his fellows; and Shrimp, John a Kent's familiar, who can make himself invisible and sound music in the air, gives us a slight foretaste of Ariel. There are some historic titles, Ranulph, Earl of Chester, and Llewellen, Prince of North Wales, among the *dramatis personae*, but the whole action takes place in a land of make-believe.

Munday goes back to biographical history, with a very liberal alloy of fiction, in *The Downfall of Robert Earl of Huntingdon*, published in 1601, for which Henslowe paid him £5 on 15 February 1598 as 'the first parte of Robyne Hoode'. By birth the hero is Robert, Earl of Huntingdon, who is betrothed to Matilda, daughter of Lord Fitzwater. Through the enmity of his uncle, the Prior of York, he is proclaimed an outlaw during the spousal banquet, and takes refuge with Marion (as Matilda is henceforth known) in Sherwood Forest, where he is joined by Little John, Friar Tuck, and other of his merry men. This is his 'downfall', though it leads to no repining:

> Marion, thou seest, though courtly pleasures want,
> Yet country sport in Sherwood is not scant.
> . . . . . .
> For arras hangings and rich tapestry
> We have sweet nature's best embroidery,
> For thy steel glass, wherein thou wont'st to look,
> Thy crystal eyes gaze in a crystal brook.
> At court a flower or two did deck thy head,
> Now with whole garlands is it circled;
> For what in wealth we want, we have in flowers,
> And what we lose in halls, we find in bowers.

But the action is only in part in the greenwood, and introduces loftier personages than the outlawed Earl. King Richard is on crusade, leaving the Bishop of Ely as his deputy but overpowered by Prince John and the Queen-mother Elinor. Historical truth is romanticized out of all seeming when John is shown as a rival for Marion's love and Elinor as enamoured of Robin. But their chief concern is to become all-powerful, and, one by one, those who stand in John's way, Ely, Fitzwater, the Prior of York, are dismissed, and find their way to Sherwood, where Robin gives hospitality to all, even those who have done him most wrong. Well may King Richard when he returns unexpectedly to claim his crown and sceptre salute Huntingdon as

> True pillar of my state, right lord indeed,
> Whose honour shineth in the day of need.

The play is further complicated by a curious enveloping plot, concerned with its rehearsal for a performance before King Henry VIII, and introducing among others the poet John Skelton, who plays Friar Tuck in the Sherwood scenes with characteristic 'ribble-rabble rhymes Skeltonical'.

Henry Chettle, already associated with Munday in *Sir Thomas More*, was paid ten shillings by Henslowe on 18 November 1598 for 'the mendynge of' the first Part of *Robin Hood*, and both dramatists had already collaborated in the second Part, published in 1601 as *The Death of Robert Earl of Huntingdon*. The title is really a misnomer, for Robin dies in the odour of sanctity at the end of the first Act, and henceforward John, who has succeeded Richard as king, is the central figure. Though he has taken unto himself as queen the noble lady Isabella, he still pursues Matilda (as she is now again called) with his lawless love till she flies to Dunmow Abbey, where she is poisoned by his villainous agent, Brand. And because her uncle, Bruce, with his elder son opposes John's designs, he barbarously starves Lady Bruce and a younger son to death in the dungeons of Windsor Castle. The four Acts are a long-drawn-out and somewhat confused display of 'the tempestuous rage of tyrant John', who shows signs of repentance only when Louis, the Dauphin of France, has invaded England, and declares to his barons

> I will be bettter than I yet have been.

Thus John had loomed large in the eyes of the writers of chronicle-history plays for over half a century. One can scarcely recognize Bale's 'noble kynge Johan' in 'the tyrant John' of Munday and Chettle's play. Between them, with a little of the patriot and a great deal of the villain, stands the John of *The Troublesome Raigne* and of Shakespeare's play. But one thing all these Tudor dramatists have in common—they make no mention of Magna Charta which for us is the central event of the reign.

IX

CHRISTOPHER MARLOWE AND POETIC TRAGEDY

SINCE the golden age of Tudor drama had been heralded by the performances of *Campaspe* and *Sapho and Phao* in 1584, it had been variously and abundantly enriched. Lyly had furnished his delicate fancy and his sparkling prose dialogue; Kyd his skilled craftsmanship and his flair for the arresting situation and phrase; the University wits their academic culture and versatile talents;[1] the writers of domestic tragedy their poignant realism, and the chronicle-history playwrights their patriotic impulse and zest for the vivid panorama of national life. But for the English theatre to attain its meridian height there was needed the supreme gift of lofty poetic imagination. This was now to be supplied by Christopher Marlowe.

Marlowe, born on 6 February 1564, was Shakespeare's senior by about eleven weeks, but we naturally think of him as a predecessor, for his career came to its close just when Shakespeare's was getting fairly under way. There is nothing more poignant in the range of Elizabethan tragic art than the untimely fate of the young poet-dramatist. New light has of late been thrown upon it from documentary sources, but every discovery has brought fresh problems in its train.

The eldest son of John Marlowe, a Canterbury shoemaker, by his marriage with Catherine Arthur, Christopher was sent for about two years to the King's School, where the educational curriculum included the

[1] See Chapter X, below.

frequent performance of plays. Hence he passed in the Lent Term 1581, with a scholarship on Archbishop Parker's foundation, to Corpus Christi College, Cambridge. His surname, after a common Elizabethan fashion, had a number of variants, Marley, Merlin, and Morley. It is as Marley that he took his B.A. degree in March 1584, and his M.A. in July 1587. But before he proceeded to the latter the Government had to intervene in a very unusual way.

Dr. Leslie Hotson, an American scholar, was the first to recognize that the following entry in the Register of the Privy Council, under date 29 June 1587, referred to the dramatist:

> Whereas it was reported that Christopher Morley was determined to haue gone beyond the seas to Reames[1] and there to remaine Their Lordships thought good to certefie that he hath no such intent, but that in all his accions he had behaued him self orderlie and discreetlie wherebie he had done her Majestie good service, and deserued to be rewarded for his faithfull dealinge: Their Lordships request that the rumor thereof should be allaied by all possible meanes, and that he should be furthered in the degree he was to take at this next Commencement: Because it was not her Majesties pleasure that anie one emploied as he had been in matters touching the benefitt of his Countrie should be defamed by those that are ignorant of th' affaires he went about.

There were other Cambridge Christopher Morleys about this time, but close examination supports the view that the dramatist is here meant. He had evidently been employed in some form of Government service, and had incurred, in some quarters, the suspicion of being anxious to join the body of English Roman Catho-

[1] i.e. Rheims.

lics at their head-quarters in Rheims. The Privy Council indignantly repudiated this allegation against him. In any case Marlowe had now given up the idea of taking orders in the Anglican Church, which had been one of the conditions attached to the Parker scholarship. We can think of him, like Doctor Faustus in his play, weighing the traditional studies in the balance and finally crying, 'Divinity, adieu!' At Cambridge he seems to have devoted himself chiefly to the classics, not in a spirit of critical scholarship, but with the ardour of a Renaissance humanist. Throughout his life he was to be haunted by visions of beauty and heroic grandeur embodied in the radiant figures of antiquity—Helen and Hero, Paris and Leander, Achilles and Alexander.

No work with his name on the title-page was published during his lifetime, and the dating of his plays and poems is therefore largely conjectural. But internal evidence suggests that his inaccurate but lively translation of Ovid's *Amores* in rhymed couplets belongs in whole or in part to his Cambridge days. With that period we may also associate the more mature blank-verse translation of Lucan's *Pharsalia*, Book I, and the original version of the play, *Dido, Queen of Carthage*, published in 1594, with the names of Marlowe and Nashe on the title-page. Whether they collaborated when they were contemporaries at Cambridge, or Nashe revised the play before it was acted by the Children of the Chapel, is uncertain. In any case Marlowe was the predominant partner in this attractive dramatization of the earlier books of the *Aeneid*. Dido, love's martyr, is drawn on a fuller scale than any other woman in Marlowe's plays, and Iarbas, the rival suitor for the queen's hand, is elaborated as a counterpoise to the faithless Aeneas.

But when Marlowe settled down in London and began to write for the Lord Admiral's men, he took as his subject not a classical figure but the Scythian conqueror, Timour or Tamburlaine, whose career ended in 1405 and whose triumphs in arms recalled those of

Tamburlaine, the great.

Tamburlaine as depicted in a woodcut at the end of Part I of Marlowe's play in the 1590, 1593, and 1597 octavos

Alexander. *Tamburlaine the Great* was published by Richard Jones in two Parts in 1590 and again in 1592. In neither edition was the name of the author given, but Marlowe's claim is sufficiently substantiated by internal evidences of style and by Robert Greene's allusion in his prefatory epistle to *Perimedes the Black-Smith* (1588) to 'that Atheist *Tamburlan*', followed by a gibe at 'the mad and scoffing poets, that have propheticall spirits, as bred of *Merlins* race'. Both Parts must have been written and acted before the letter of 10 November 1587 mentioned below, concerned with an episode in Act V of Part II.

Marlowe was indebted for the details of the Scythian's career to half a dozen authorities, in particular the Spaniard Pedro Mexia's *Silva*, freely translated from a French version by Thomas Fortescue, and the Latin *Life* by Petrus Perondinus. The geographical details of his campaigns, long looked upon as merely fantastic, have recently been shown to be based upon the contemporary map of Ortelius, *Theatrum Orbis Terrarum.*[1] And an investigation of current Elizabethan psychological and physiological conceptions proves that Marlowe followed them closely in his portraiture of the Scythian.

But the increased realization of the dramatist's fidelity to his sources only throws into further relief his profoundly original transformation of them. Tamburlaine is no longer merely a stupendous Oriental conqueror. He becomes the embodiment of the elemental desires that swept tumultuously through the young poet's soul, the intoxicating, insatiable craving for power and beauty and knowledge.

Thus Tamburlaine's impassioned quest of universal sovereignty is no mere vulgar lust of rule. When in Act II, Sc. vi, he has defeated Cosroe, the Persian, who with his dying breath upbraids him as 'barbarous and bloody Tamburlaine', he justifies himself by the example of Jupiter in dethroning Saturn:

> The thirst of reign and sweetness of a crown,
> That caused the eldest son of heavenly Ops

[1] See 'Marlowe's Map', by Ethel Seaton, in English Association *Essays and Studies*, vol. x (1924).

To thrust his doting father from his chair,
And place himself in the empyreal heaven,
Mov'd me to manage arms against thy state.
What better precedent than mighty Jove?

As he proceeds from triumph to triumph, the Olympians themselves acknowledge him their superior (v. ii):

The God of war resigns his room to me,
Meaning to make me General of the world;
Jove viewing me in arms looks pale and wan,
Fearing my power should pull him from his throne.

This is Tamburlaine's exulting cry to the Soldan of Egypt, father of the fair captive Zenocrate who has won his love, and who is afflicted by his assault upon her native soil. Her tears 'lay siege' unto his soul and move him to a rhapsody on beauty itself more beautiful than had been heard on any stage since the last accents of Euripides:

What is beauty? saith my sufferings then.
If all the pens that ever poets held
Had fed the feeling of their masters' thoughts,
And every sweetness that inspired their hearts
Their minds and muses on admired themes,
If all the heavenly quintessence they still
From their immortal flowers of poesy,
Wherein as in a mirror we perceive
The highest reaches of a human wit,
If these had made one poem's period,
And all combined in beauty's worthiness,
Yet should there hover in their restless heads
One thought, one grace, one wonder at the least
Which into words no virtue can digest.

This lyrical outburst is as characteristic of Marlowe, and as ill-fitted to the lips of the Scythian conqueror, as his earlier linking of his ambitions 'urge' with the intellectual impulse that would unlock the secrets of the cosmos (II. vii):

> Nature that framed us of four elements,
> Warring within our breasts for regiment,
> Doth teach us all to have aspiring minds:
> Our souls, whose faculties can comprehend
> The wondrous architecture of the world,
> And measure every wandering planet's course
> Still climbing after knowledge infinite
> And always moving as the restless spheres
> Wills us to wear ourselves and never rest,
> Until we reach the ripest fruit of all
> That perfect bliss and sole felicity,
> The sweet fruition of an earthly crown.

And it is this philosopher-poet who (to the complete satisfaction of the audiences in Henslowe's theatres) violates all dramatic consistency by massacring the suppliant virgins of Damascus, and using as his footstool the captive Turkish Soldan Bajazeth, whom he carries about in a cage till he beats out his brains against the wires.

In Part II it is this aspect of Tamburlaine as the savage warrior that becomes predominant. We hear again his poetic voice, as his queen lies on her deathbed, in the exquisite strophic threnody beginning (II. iii):

> Now walk the angels on the walls of heaven,
> As sentinels to warn th' immortal souls
> To entertain divine Zenocrate.

and in the classical echo, as lovely as it is irrelevant:

> And had she lived before the siege of Troy,
> Helen, whose beauty summoned Greece to arms,
> And drew a thousand ships to Tenedos,
> Had not been named in Homer's *Iliads*.

But he lays in ashes the town in which she dies; he stabs his eldest son to death because he is faint of heart (IV. i); he harnesses the captured kings of Trebizon and Soria to his chariot with bits in their mouths; and in a passage that became as notorious as any of Hieronimo's outbursts in *The Spanish Tragedy*, he cries (IV. iii):

> Holla, ye pampered jades of Asia!
> What! can ye draw but twenty miles a day,
> And have so proud a chariot at your heels,
> And such a coachman as great Tamburlaine?

When the city of Babylon falls before him he hangs up the Governor in chains on the walls for the soldiers to shoot at him. This piece of dramatic ferocity resulted in an actual fatality, not to the Governor, but to a child in the theatre who, as we learn from a letter written on 10 November 1587, was killed accidentally, by a shot fired by one of the Lord Admiral's players in this scene. Finally Tamburlaine orders every man, woman, and child in the city to be drowned in the neighbouring lake. But Death who has so long been his obsequious henchman is at last, when he lies stricken with sickness, to prove his master (V. iii):

> See, where my slave, the ugly monster, Death,
> Shaking and quivering, pale and wan for fear,
> Stands aiming at me with his murdering dart,
> Who flies away at every glance I give,
> And, when I look away, comes stealing on.

He summons up his strength for a final victorious encounter with the son of Bajazeth, and then feeling that his martial strength is spent, shows to his two surviving sons on a map the extent of his own conquests and what 'a world of ground' is left them to subdue.

Even Death is robbed of half his victory when with his last breath Tamburlaine invests his heir with the symbols of royalty, and bids him be his second self:

> So reign, my son, scourge and control those slaves,
> Guiding thy chariot with thy father's hand.

The cosmopolitan atmosphere of *Tamburlaine* is reproduced in *The Jew of Malta*, which, as the large number of performances recorded by Henslowe testifies, achieved a popularity at least equal to that of the earlier two-part play. The first of Henslowe's entries is on 26 February 1591/2, when it was acted by Lord Strange's men, though not as a new play. Its composition must lie between that date and 23 December 1588, the date of the Duke of Guise's death, mentioned in line 3 of the Prologue. It probably belongs to 1589–90 and is linked to *Tamburlaine* not only by its cosmopolitanism but by what its latest editor has called 'the impetuous violence' of its plot.

It is uncertain where Marlowe sought the prototype of his Barabas. In the Latin Chronicle of Turkish affairs by Philip Lonicerus (1584), one of his sources for *Tamburlaine*, he may have read about Juan Migues, a Portuguese Jew, who settled in Constantinople about 1555, and became the powerful favourite of Sultan Selim II. Or he may have been acquainted, through his government service or otherwise, with the career of a later Jew of Constantinople, David Passi, who became involved in the Turkish designs on Malta and whose projects ended in failure early in 1591. In any case Marlowe stamped his own creative genius on the figure of his wealthy Jew. As we see him first he is a Tamburlaine, or in modern phraseology, a Napoleon of finance, to whom his treasury of jewels and his ships laden with precious cargoes are as potent instruments as his armies to a conqueror:

Bags of fiery opals, sapphires, amethysts,
Jacinths, hard topaz, grass-green emeralds,
Beauteous rubies, sparkling diamonds,
And seld-seen costly stones . . .
This is the ware wherein consists my wealth.

. . . .

I hope my ships
I sent for Egypt and the bordering isles
Are gotten up by Nilus' winding banks:
Mine argosy from Alexandria,
Loaden with spice and silks, now under sail,
Are smoothly gliding down by Candy-shore,
To Malta, through our Mediterranean sea.

Indeed when Barabas is despoiled at a blow of all his wealth by the Governor of Malta, to meet the demand of the Turks for ten years' arrears of tribute, he pictures himself to his countrymen as a defeated general (I. ii):

But give him liberty at least to mourn,
That in a field, amidst his enemies,
Doth see his soldiers slain, himself disarm'd,
And knows no means of his recovery:
Ay, let me sorrow for this sudden chance;
'Tis in the trouble of my spirit I speak:
Great injuries are not so soon forgot.

As a vanquished soldier of fortune he is not without dignity and pathos, but he forfeits our sympathy, though not our interest, when, to regain his position of affluence, he has recourse to the 'policy' of Machiavelli (as vulgarly interpreted) who in the Prologue appears to present the play, with the declaration,

I count religion but a childish toy,
And hold there is no sin but ignorance.

In this spirit, as his house has been converted into a nunnery, he persuades his daughter Abigail to become a novice, that she may fling down to him by night hidden bags of jewels, while he cries in alliterative ecstasy (echoed later in Shylock's 'my daughter and my ducats')

> O girl! O gold! O beauty! O my bliss!

Barabas does not, however, show himself the complete Machiavellian till he buys in the slave-market Ithamore, who is his rival in every villainous practice. So *naif* indeed is their mutual confession of their nefarious deeds (II. iii), and so grotesque Ithamore's cry, with reference to the Jew's stage make-up,

> O brave master! I worship your nose for this,

that there are modern critics who take the view that Marlowe is here deliberately burlesquing the Machiavellian type of villain. But this is to over-subtilize the dramatist's own genius and the mentality of the Elizabethan 'groundlings'. There was no intellectual refinement in their full-blooded enjoyment, which we cannot fully share to-day, of the Jew's machinations, with Ithamore as his instrument, to repair his fortunes and have revenge on his enemies. He contrives that his daughter's two Christian lovers, of whom one is the Governor's son, shall kill one another. When Abigail thereupon re-enters the convent, he poisons her and the rest of the nuns. He strangles the friar to whom in confession she has revealed his guilt, and by a stratagem, with Ithamore as his accomplice, contrives that another friar shall think himself accountable for the murder. Betrayed by Ithamore, who reveals his villanies, he is arrested, but feigns death, and is flung over the city walls, where he is found by the Turks who have again invaded the island.

In return for information that helps them to capture the city they make him Governor, but he thinks it more profitable to come to terms again with the Maltese and to lure the Turkish leaders to a death-trap in the citadel and the rank and file to massacre by an explosion in a monastery. The massacre goes according to plan, but the former Governor by cutting the cord of the trap before the time causes Barabas to fall into the pit prepared for the Turkish chiefs, containing a heated cauldron, the 'j caudern for the Jewe', noted by Henslowe among the theatrical properties of the Admiral's men in March 1598. We can imagine the jeering roars of the Elizabethan theatrical crowd as the bottle-nosed Barabas hurled from the cauldron his last curses on his enemies:

> Had I but escap'd this stratagem,
> I would have brought confusion on you all,
> Damn'd Christians, dogs,[1] and Turkish infidels!
> But now begins the extremity of heat
> To pinch me with intolerable pangs:
> Die, life! fly, soul! tongue, curse thy fill, and die!

The later Acts of *The Jew of Malta* contain few of those highly wrought poetic passages which to us represent the essential Marlowe. But, especially with such an actor as Edward Alleyn in the title-role, they were good 'theatre', and they account for the enduring success of the play upon the boards. Strangely enough, though it was entered on the Stationers' Register on 17 May 1594, there is no copy extant previous to the quarto edition of 1633 which contained Prologues and Epilogues written by Thomas Heywood for the presentation of the play before the King and Queen at Whitehall and at the *Cockpit* Theatre in Drury Lane. It has been suggested that Heywood otherwise edited the play, and it is true

[1] The reading of the quarto, perhaps a mistake for 'Christian dogs'.

that the episode of the two Friars resembles one in his manuscript piece *The Captives*. But neither in his epistle dedicatory, nor in either of the Prologues, does he hint that he has altered a piece

> writ many years agone,
> And in that age thought second unto none.

Indeed the apologies that he makes for presenting this antiquated work at Court ' 'mongst other plays that in fashion are' indicate that Heywood was reviving it in what he thought to be its original form.

In Marlowe's own Prologue to *The Jew of Malta* Machiavelli had announced that his soul had flown beyond the Alps and had first become embodied in the Guise. In *The Massacre at Paris* not only the Duke of Guise, but the Queen-mother Catherine de Medici, and the Duke of Anjou, afterwards Henry III, show themselves as complete Machiavellians as Barabas and Ithamore. The play was acted as new at the *Rose* Theatre on 26 January 1592/3. As it ends with the death of King Henry III on 2 August 1587 and alludes to the 'bones' of Pope Sixtus V, who died on 17 August 1590, it may be approximately dated 1591–2. The only edition, an octavo, is undated and presents a corrupt text. If a fragment, containing one short scene, printed by J. P. Collier in 1825 is genuine, the octavo text of about 1,200 lines would seem to have been considerably abbreviated. In any case the work is the most unsatisfactorily episodic among Marlowe's plays, and the one in which the raw material has been least transformed by his genius. Yet this dramatic version of contemporary French history, beginning with the marriage between Henry of Navarre and Margaret of Valois in August 1572, has gained increased interest from the recent discovery that

Marlowe was for a time engaged in Government service, and had been suspected of a desire to take up his residence with the English Romanists at Rheims. Had he this in mind when he makes it one of the charges against the Guise (scene xviii):

> Did he not draw a sort of English priest,
> From Douai to the seminary at Rheims,
> To hatch forth treason 'gainst their natural queen?

The Duke's fanatical Catholicism differentiates him from other Marlovian protagonists. But blended with this is the limitless ambition of a Tamburlaine (scene ii):

> Give me a look, that, when I bend the brows,
> Pale death may walk in furrows of my face;
> A hand, that with a grasp may gripe the world . . .
> A royal seat, a sceptre, and a crown;
> That those which do behold, they[1] may become
> As men that stand and gaze against the sun,

coupled with a ruthless Machiavellian 'policy' that sticks at nothing, from poisoning an aged queen with perfumed gloves, to organizing the massacre of St. Bartholomew and levying war against his own sovereign Henry III, who finally over-reaches him at his own game of treacherous assassination. The King in turn suffers the same fate at the hands of a Jacobin friar, but lives long enough to send warning to Elizabeth to beware of similar treachery, and to urge his successor, Henry of Navarre, to revenge his death on 'that wicked Church of Rome'. Marlowe had certainly no historical justification for putting these Protestant sentiments into Henry III's mouth, while Henry of Navarre, so far from seeking vengeance on 'Rome and all those Popish

[1] The reading of the quarto, perhaps a mistake for 'behold them'.

prelates there', about a month after the dramatist's own death became a convert to Catholicism.

As *Edward II* was acted, not by the Lord Admiral's, but by the Earl of Pembroke's men, Henslowe's *Diary* does not help us to date it. The play was not entered in the Stationers' Register till July 1593, a month after Marlowe's death, and the first extant quarto was published in 1594. It probably followed rather than preceded *The Massacre at Paris*, with which it has closer links that have been always recognized. Henry III in *The Massacre* is a pleasure-loving king, delighting in

> barriers, tourney, tilt,
> And like disports such as do fit a court,

and putting his trust in his 'minions', Epernoun and Joyeux, while the great nobles abetted by the Queen-mother form an opposing faction. Similarly Edward II lavishes his affections on favourites, Gaveston and Spencer, who minister to his aesthetic susceptibilities. As the former soliloquizes (I. i):

> I must have wanton poets, pleasant wits,
> Musicians that with touching of a string
> May draw the pliant king which way I please:
> Music and poetry is his delight;
> Therefore I'll have Italian masks by night,
> Sweet speeches, comedies, and pleasing shows.

Ranged in angry opposition are the barons, headed by the Earl of Warwick and the younger Mortimer, who draws to himself the affections of the slighted Queen Isabel, herself a member of the ill-fated house of Valois. Even the feud in *The Massacre* between the monarchy and the Church has its parallel in *Edward II*, for the Archbishop of Canterbury, as Papal Legate, enforces the banishment of Gaveston, and Edward echoes the last words of Henry in an outburst that Bale might have put into the mouth of his King Johan:

> Why should a king be subject to a priest?
> Proud Rome, that hatchest such imperial grooms,
> For these thy superstitious taperlights,
> Wherewith thy antichristian churches blaze,
> I'll fire thy crazed buildings and enforce
> The papal towers to kiss the lowly ground.

But though in its general grouping and atmosphere *Edward II* has much in common with *The Massacre*, it is immeasurably superior in characterization, in constructive power and swift and pregnant dialogue. Gaveston, the frivolous fop, who, in outlandish fashion,

> wears a short Italian hooded cloak
> Larded with pearl and in his Tuscan cap
> A jewel of more value than the crown,

is hit off in deft strokes. When Warwick, his bitterest foe among the barons, by a ruse brings about his death, Edward vows revenge in the traditional Senecan style:

> By earth, the common mother of us all,
> By heaven and all the moving orbs thereof,
> By this right hand, and by my father's sword,
> And all the honours 'longing to my crown,
> I will have heads and lives for him as many
> As I have manors, castles, towns and towers.
> Treacherous Warwick, traitorous Mortimer,
> If I be England's king, in lakes of gore
> Your headless trunks, your bodies will I trail.

But it is by pity, not terror as in the previous plays, that Marlowe now rises to the height of his tragic achievement. Overpowered by his enemies, Edward takes refuge in the Abbey at Neath, which to his mercurial fancy seems a haven of rest:

> Father, this life contemplative is heaven,
> O that I might this life in quiet lead!
> . . . good father, on thy lap
> Lay I this head laden with mickle care;
> O might I never ope these eyes again,
> Never again lift up this drooping head,
> O never more lift up this dying heart!

Yet when he is removed to Kenilworth Castle and ordered to resign the crown in favour of his son, Prince Edward, he clings to the emblem of sovereignty:

> Here take my crown, the life of Edward too,
> Two kings in England cannot reign at once:
> But stay a while, let me be king till night,
> That I may gaze upon this glittering crown.

With another swift change of mood he hears that he must depart for Berkeley Castle:

> Whither you will: all places are alike,
> And every earth is fit for burial.

The closing scenes in the gloomy castle vaults are a pitifully ironic answer to Tamburlaine's exultant cry, 'Is it not brave to be a king?'

> This dungeon where they keep me is the sink,
> Wherein the filth of all the castle falls.
> And there in mire and puddle have I stood
> This ten days' space, and lest that I should sleep,
> One plays continually upon a drum:
> They give me bread and water being a king . . .
> O would my blood dropped out from every vein,
> As doth this water from my tattered robes!

And it is the supreme touch of irony that this is spoken by Edward to Lightborn, sent by Mortimer to murder him. He is a villain of Ithamore's breed who has learnt in Naples the various arts of how to kill a man without leaving an outward sign. But his secret crime accomplished, he is at once dispatched by order of Mortimer, who in his turn is betrayed to the young King by one of Edward's jailers, and sentenced to the savage doom of hanging and quartering. But these deeds of blood are not, as at the close of *The Massacre*, parts of a crude catastrophe. They are the *dénouement* of an organic plot in which Marlowe's genius has lifted the chronicle-history into the sphere of tragic art.

But it was not among the captains and the kings, of East or West, that this genius was to find its most congenial subject. Soon after his arrival in London Marlowe had gained a reputation for 'atheism'. It was a loosely-used term, like radicalism, socialism, and bolshevism in later days, to denote opinions hostile to the orthodox moral and political system. But there are still extant among the British Museum manuscripts and documents two letters of Thomas Kyd to Sir John Puckering, the Lord Keeper, and a 'Note' by an in-informer, Richard Baines, which make detailed charges against Marlowe of revolutionary and blasphemous utterances. Whether these be taken literally or not, there can be no doubt that he had a restlessly inquiring intellect, critical of all the accepted bases of belief, ecclesiastical or civil. He was thus naturally attracted by the story of Doctor John Faustus, the Wittenberg scholar and necromancer who, in pursuit of forbidden fruits of knowledge and pleasure, had sold his soul to the Devil. The story had become popularized in the German *Faust Book*, published at Frankfort in 1587. An English translation by 'P. F.' appeared in 1592, and new bibliographical evidence has made it almost certain that no edition was issued before that year. As Marlowe closely followed P. F.'s version in his play, *The Tragical History of Doctor Faustus*, this is probably to be assigned to 1592, though it has been usual to date it somewhat earlier. The first performance recorded by Henslowe, though not of it as a new play, was at the *Rose* on 30 September 1594. It was entered on the Stationers' Register on 7 January 1600/1 by Thomas Bushell, but he apparently did not bring out an edition till 1604. This was a quarto of about 1,500 lines, considerably shorter than any of Marlowe's other plays except *Dido* and *The Massacre*. In 1616 an enlarged edition was published by Thomas Wright with some 550 additional lines. This preserves some fragments of Marlowe's work omitted in the 1604 quarto, but the additions appear to be mainly from the hand of Samuel Rowley, to whom, with William Birde, Henslowe had on 22 November 1602 paid £4 'for ther adicyones in doctor Fostes'.

Whether or not the 1604 *Doctor Faustus* has been abridged, it includes the most significant episodes in the English *Faust Book*, and Marlowe went still farther than P. F., who had called Faustus 'the insatiable speculator', in laying stress upon his intellectual curiosity. It is true that Faustus, when by the aid of his necromantic books he has summoned Mephistophilis to his side, cries in the spirit of Tamburlaine (I. iii):

> By him I'll be great Emperor of the world,
> And make a bridge through the moving air,
> To pass the ocean with a band of men;
> I'll join the hills that bind the Afric shore,
> And make that country continent to Spain,
> And both contributory to my crown.

But in his dialogue with Mephistophilis he is most

deeply concerned with the question of the fallen angel's present state:

> *Faust.* Where are you damn'd?
> *Meph.* In hell.
> *Faust.* How comes it then that thou art out of hell?
> *Meph.* Why this is hell, nor am I out of it.
> Think'st thou that I who saw the face of God,
> And tasted the eternal joys of heaven,
> Am not tormented with ten thousand hells
> In being depriv'd of everlasting bliss?

Thus the 'atheist' Marlowe in these lines, of which there is no hint in his source, gives a spiritual interpretation of hell that must have fallen strangely upon the ears of the groundlings in the *Rose* Theatre. And after he has signed the fatal bond which commits him, after twenty-four years, body and soul to Lucifer, he again returns to the problem of hell, and later to questions of 'divine astrology' on which Mephistophilis discourses with specialist knowledge. It is in such scenes and not in the conjuring episodes in Acts III and IV at the Courts of the Pope, the Emperor, and the Duke of Anholt, based on the English *Faust Book*, and expanded in the 1616 quarto, that the essential Faustus of Marlowe is found. But these conjuring episodes, when compared with their source, are seen to have more theatrical value and coherence than has been often recognized, while the Wagner and Robin scenes provide something of a comic parallel to the main plot.

With the vision of Helen of Troy in Act V, Marlowe recaptures, and intensifies, the glorious lyrical strain with which Tamburlaine had hymned Zenocrate:

> Was this the face that launch'd a thousand ships,
> And burnt the topless towers of Ilium?
> Sweet Helen, make me immortal with a kiss!

Her lips suck forth my soul: see where it flies!
Come, Helen, come, give me my soul again.
Here will I dwell, for heaven is in these lips,
And all is dross that is not Helena.

And close upon this superb invocation follows Marlowe's masterpiece of prose, the dialogue between Faustus and the scholars as on his last night he awaits the coming of Lucifer (v. ii):

Sec. Schol. Yet, Faustus, look up to heaven; remember God's mercies are infinite.

Faust. But Faustus' offence can ne'er be pardoned; the serpent that tempted Eve may be saved, but not Faustus. . . . O would I had never seen Wittenberg, never read book! and what wonders I have done, all Germany can witness, yea, all the world; for which Faustus hath lost both Germany and the world; yea, heaven itself, heaven, the seat of God, the throne of the blessed, the kingdom of joy; and must remain in hell for ever—hell, oh, hell for ever.

The pathos is even more poignant here than in the highly wrought soliloquy, where Marlowe's lyrical and dramatic powers are perfectly fused, with which Faustus seeks to prolong his last hour. Of all his outcries the most agonizing is that in which he curses his own immortality:

Let Faustus live in hell a thousand years,
A hundred thousand and at last be sav'd!
O, no end is limited to damned souls!
Why wert thou not a creature wanting soul?
Or why is this immortal that thou hast?

It is just because Faustus, even after he has sold himself to the devil, is 'not a creature wanting soul', not a mere pleasure-lover, but a seeker after knowledge and beauty, that his is in the deepest sense a 'tragical history'.

Marlowe hymned Helen in twenty incomparable lines. Two other radiant figures of antiquity, Hero and Leander, had won from him the tribute of over eight hundred lines of exquisitely flowing narrative verse, when his hand was suddenly arrested for ever. It was probably owing to the charges brought against him by Kyd that the Privy Council ordered on 18 May 1593 that Marlowe, who was then at the house of Thomas Walsingham, near Chislehurst, should be brought before them. What further steps they took, or intended to take, is not known. But on 30 May the dramatist spent the day at Eleanor Bull's tavern in Deptford with three associates of sinister reputation, Robert Poley, a noted spy and informer, and Ingram Frizer and Nicholas Skeres, who had been mixed up in shady financial transactions. According to the story that was accepted on 1 June by the Coroner's jury, there was a quarrel after supper about 'le recknynge' (the bill), during which Marlowe attacked Frizer, who killed him in self-defence. Whether there was a deeper, personal or political, cause for the affray, and whether Marlowe was in truth the first assailant, are hotly debated problems to which, on our present evidence, there is no conclusive answer.

But 'whatever record leap to light', and however the man Christopher Marlowe be now or hereafter judged, his genius, within less than thirty stormy years, lit up the English theatre with a novel and fiery splendour which, after the dramatic revolutions of well-nigh three centuries and a half, has suffered no shadow of eclipse.

X

THE UNIVERSITY WITS AND THEIR EXPERIMENTS

WHILE Lyly, Kyd, and Marlowe were preparing the way for Shakespeare's crowning work, a group of contemporaries who have been conveniently termed 'the University Wits' were making contributions to Tudor drama, of which none was in itself of first-rate significance, but which collectively make a notable addition to its variety and range. These 'wits' were graduates of Oxford or Cambridge, who threw themselves into the literary life of the capital as poets, pamphleteers, novelists, and satirists, and were playwrights on occasion, not exploring any distinctively original path, but experimenting in different styles. Robert Greene's account in his pamphlet, *A Groatsworth of Wit*, of how he began to write plays, may be taken as at least symbolically true, not only of himself but of his associates. When his fortunes were at their lowest, and he was sitting down by a hedge to lament his fate, he was overheard by a player, who declared that he would do his best to procure him profit or bring him pleasure. Roberto, as Greene calls himself, then asked, 'How mean you to use me?' 'Why, sir,' answered the other, 'in making plays, for which you will be well paid, if you will take the pains.' Thereupon 'Roberto, perceiving no remedy, thought best in respect of his present necessity to try his wit and went with him willingly'.

Though George Peele was of higher social origin than Greene, he too had been in financial straits before he began to write plays in the Capital. Born in London about 1558, and son of the Clerk of Christ's Hospital, he was educated there and at Broadgates Hall (now Pembroke College) and Christ Church, Oxford. He was in residence for ten years, and towards the end of this period, in October 1580, made an improvident marriage with a young Oxford girl, Anna Christian, and found himself in money difficulties. But, according to Anthony Wood, 'he was esteemed a most noted poet in the University', this reputation being based on an early work, afterwards revised, *A Tale of Troy*, and on a translation of one of the *Iphigenia* plays by Euripides, performed in Christ Church hall.

Classical subjects thus attracted him from the first, and when he came to London early in 1581, and wrote a play for the Children of the Chapel to be acted before the Queen, he naturally chose an episode from the Trojan legend, though he gave it an ingenious topical turn. *The Arraignment of Paris* (published in 1584) is closely linked with Lyly's court comedies in its mythological theme and in the circumstances of its performance. But it differs from them in one feature of the highest importance—it is written not in prose but in verse. Few plays can show a greater medley of metres, suggesting that Peele was deliberately trying experiments. The prologue, spoken by Ate and foreshadowing 'the tragedy of Troy', is in blank verse. The opening scene, wherein the floral deities make ready to welcome Juno, Pallas, and Venus on Mount Ida, is partly in five-foot rhymed couplets, partly in the long 'fourteeners'. So also in the scene that follows between Paris and Oenone (I. ii), and in the dialogue (II. i) between the goddesses when each claims the golden apple that has been 'trundled' to their feet. The speech of Pallas illustrates Peele's lucid and fluent verse:

To stand on terms of beauty, as you take it,
Believe me, ladies, is but to mistake it.
The beauty that this subtle prize must win,
No outward beauty hight, but dwells within;
And sift it as you please, and you shall find
This beauty is the beauty of the mind.

. . . .

And look how much the mind, the better part,
Doth overpass the body in desert,
So much the mistress of these gifts divine
Excels thy beauty, and that state of thine.
Then, if this prize be thus bequeathed to beauty,
The only she that wins this prize am I.

But Venus, with a show of 'Helen in her bravery', attended by four Cupids, and singing an Italian song, wins the reward from Paris. His desertion of Oenone is contrasted in Act III with the faithful and unhappy love of Colin for Thestylis, suggested by Spenser's recently published *Shepherd's Calendar*. But he regains our sympathies when he is summoned, at the suit of Juno and Pallas, before the Council of the Gods and

arraigned of partiality,
Of sentence partial and unjust; for that without indifferency,
Beyond desert or merit far, as these accusers say,
From them to Lady Venus here thou gav'st the prize away.

His 'oration' to the Olympian court is in nearly one hundred lines of resonant blank verse, which had hitherto been confined, as far as we know, to the Inns of Court stage and which must have taxed the elocutionary powers of the Chapel boy who played Paris. It is thus that he puts his final plea:

Suppose I gave, and judged corruptly then
For hope of that that best did please my thought.

. . . .

And tempted more than ever creature was
With wealth, with beauty, and with chivalry,
And so preferred beauty before them all,
The thing that hath enchanted heaven itself.
And for the one, contentment is my wealth;
A shell of salt will serve a shepherd swain.

. . . .

For arms they dread no foes that sit so low;
A thorn can keep the wind from off my back,
A sheep-cote thatched a shepherd's-palace hight.

The debate among the gods that follows is in five-foot couplets, but when, on Apollo's motion, Diana gives judgement, she too speaks in blank verse. And by an audacious 'variation' upon the classical myth she awards the apple to the 'gracious nymph', Eliza—the Queen who was watching the play. The rival goddesses acquiesce in the verdict, after which the three Fates lay their 'properties' at her feet. Stage-flattery, far more open than anything attempted by Lyly, here reaches its climax. But this was in the fashion of the time, and the play deservedly won the praise of Thomas Nashe, when he wrote of Peele:

> I dare commend him unto all that know him as the chief supporter of pleasaunce now living . . . whose first increase, the *Arraignment of Paris*, might plead to your opinions his present dexterity of wit and manifold variety of invention.

If Peele was never quite to fulfil as a dramatist the high promise of his 'first increase', it was in part because of the 'manifold variety of invention' with which Nashe credits him. His versatile ease led him hither and thither in dramatic experiment. In its medley of episodes and styles *The Old Wives' Tale*, published in 1595, is somewhat akin to *The Arraignment of Paris*, but its construction is so loose, that it has been aptly compared to a modern revue, which it also resembles in its burlesque elements. Some wanderers who have lost their way in a wood are welcomed by Clunch, the smith, to his cottage where Madge, his wife, begins to entertain them with a merry winter's tale of a king's daughter carried off by a conjurer. After this introductory scene, written in lustily vernacular prose, the characters in Madge's story suddenly begin to appear on the stage to tell her tale for her. First come the two brothers of the Princess Delia, held in thrall by the conjurer Sacrapant, who with a potion has 'made her to forget herself', and who by his arts now takes captive the brothers and sets them to labour with spade and mattock, while Delia, bereft of her true senses, goads them on to work. If Peele's piece was later than *Doctor Faustus*, Sacrapant crying 'adeste, demones' to his attendant Furies, may have been a variation on Marlowe's enchanter and Mephistophilis. In any case there is a deliberate burlesque of another supernatural element in Tudor drama, the Ghost, in the scenes which lead to the liberation of the captives. Eumenides, the lover of Delia, gives his last shillings for the burial-fee of a pauper, Jack, whose Ghost in gratitude enters his service, defeats the arts of Sacrapant, cuts off his head, and reunites Eumenides to Delia. Thereupon the Ghost 'leaps down in the ground', and, in a closing scrap of rustic chat one of the wanderers asks, 'Then ye have made an end of your tale, gammer?', to which Madge answers, 'Yes, faith: when this was done, I took a piece of bread and cheese and came my way; and so shall you have too, before you go to your breakfast'. What a different *finale* from the Epilogue spoken by the Spirit with which Milton ends *Comus*, which inevitably recalls, and probably borrowed something from, the main theme of *The Old Wives' Tale*. But mixed with this, almost incoherently, are other episodes and personages, including a giant, Huanebango, whose exploits are of less interest than his parody of the hexameters of the English classicist school of versifiers:

Philida, phileridos, pamphilida, florida, flortos:
Dub dub-a-dub, bounce, quoth the guns, with a sulphurous huff-snuff:
Waked with a wench, pretty peat, pretty love and my sweet prettie pigsnie
Just by thy side shall sit surnamed great Huanebango:
Safe in my arms will I keep thee, threat Mars, or thunder Olympus.

Peele's excursion into the supernatural is not without a fantastic attraction that is lacking in his adventure into chronicle-history with *Edward I* (published 1593). It combines, in its author's characteristically loose fashion, the episodes of the return of Edward Longshanks from the Holy Land, the rebellion of Llewellyn, Prince of Wales, and the legendary sinking of Queen Elinor at Charing Cross. It is probably due to the violent anti-Spanish feeling in the period following the Armada that Peele is guilty of a libel on the fair name of Elinor which may almost rank with that on Joan of Arc in *King Henry VI*, Part I. In spite of some resounding patriotic speeches, *Edward I* shows less of Peele's gifts than any other of his plays.

There is more of interest, from several points of view, in *The Battle of Alcazar*, published anonymously in 1594, but ascribed to Peele in the anthology, *England's Parnassus* (1600), and bearing the stamp of his diction and episodic construction. The play is a variation of that type of chronicle-history, of which illustrations have been given in the later pages of Chapter VIII, where the central figure is not a royal personage, but some eminent statesman or dignitary. Here the leading role is filled by Thomas Stukeley, a Devonshire man, who played a stirring part in the affairs of Portugal and of Morocco, and who died heroically in Barbary on the field of Alcazar. With the aid of a 'presenter' and dumb-shows the episodes are loosely strung into a lively piece, which was probably acted by Lord Strange's men on various occasions from 21 February 1592 to 20 January 1593.

The quarto of 1594 does not, however, appear to give the complete text. There has been preserved a manuscript 'plot' of the play, an analysis of the entries and exits of the characters, with additions of the actors who filled the various roles and of the properties required. This document is mutilated, and the portion corresponding with Act V has been lost, but it implies a longer version of the play than the 1594 text which probably represents an abridgement used on a provincial tour. The 'plot', from the names of the cast, must relate to a revival, presumably of the original version, at the end of 1597 or later.

Peele was to make yet another experiment in a dramatic type which was attempted by few of the later Tudor playwrights. *The Love of David and Fair Bethsabe, With the Tragedy of Absalon* (published in 1599), is based upon the eleventh and following chapters of the second Book of Samuel. It has the unique interest of a scriptural play decked out with florid Renaissance ornament and cast in the mould of a Revenge tragedy. The love of David and Bethsabe (Bathsheba), though it furnishes the main title, is of secondary interest. It gives Peele the opportunity of putting into the lips of David, when he views Bethsabe 'bathing over a spring', a pleasantly ornate rhapsody:

What tree, what shade, what spring, what paradise
Enjoys the beauty of so fair a dame?
Fair Eva, placed in perfect happiness,
Lending her praise-notes to the liberal heavens,
Struck with the accents of archangels' tunes
Wrought not more pleasure to her husband's thoughts
Than this fair woman's words and notes to mine.

And the king's ecstatic outburst when she is being brought into his presence:

Now comes my lover tripping like the roe
. . . .
Open the doors and entertain my love;
Open, I say, and as you open, sing,
'Welcome, fair Bethsabe, King David's darling,'

sounds like a graceful echo, without the rich Marlovian music, of Tamburlaine's rhapsodies over the beauty of Zenocrates.

Similarly there are echoes of Kyd and his school in Peele's handling of the tragedy of David's children, which forms the body of the play. Thamar, the victim of her half-brother Amnon's (Ammon's) lust, vows that she will fly to desert woods (I. iii):

There will I lure with my windy sighs
Night-ravens and owls to rend my bloody side,
Which with a rusty weapon I will wound,
And make them passage to my panting heart.

When she reveals her monstrous secret to her brother Absalon (Absalom), he predicts the vengeance of Jehovah:

This fact[1] hath Jacob's ruler seen from heaven,
And through a cloud of smoke and tower of fire,
As he rides vaunting him upon the greens,
Shall tear his chariot-wheels with violent winds,
And throw his body in the bloody sea.

[1] Criminal deed.

And to make the prophecy sure, he stabs Amnon at a sheep-shearing. Unmoved by David's clemency he aims at his throne. And again we seem to hear the voice of Tamburlaine, strangely mingled with that of a self-proclaimed agent of Jehovah, as Absalon declares (III. ii) that he

is set in fair Jerusalem
With complete state and glory of a crown.
Fifty fair footmen by my chariot run
And to the air whose rapture rings my fame
Where'er I ride they offer reverence.
Why should not Absalon, that in his face
Carries the final purpose of his God,
. . . .
Endeavour to achieve with all his strength
The state that most may satisfy his joy,
Keeping his statutes and his covenants pure?
His thunder is entangled in my hair,
And with my beauty is his lightning quenched.

Even then David sentimentalizes, with grotesque sensuous imagery, over the beauty of his revolted son (II. iii):

Friend him with deeds, and touch no hair of him,
Not that fair hair with which the wanton winds
Delight to play, and love to make it curl,
Wherein the nightingales would build their nests,
And make sweet bowers in every golden tress,
To sing their lover every night asleep.

And when 'that fair hair' proves his undoing, David after his first outburst of grief and wrath, finds consolation in a vision of Absalon translated to a semi-Platonic, semi-Christian, heaven (IV. ii):

Thy soul shall joy the sacred cabinet
Of those divine ideas that present
Thy changed spirit with a heaven of bliss.
. . . .

Thou shall behold thy sovereign face to face,
With wonder, knit in triple unity,
Uniting infinite and innumerable.

It is not surprising that Peele's facile and graceful pen was also employed upon mayorial and other pageants and entertainments between 1585 and 1595. His *Anglorum Feriae*, written to celebrate the anniversary of the Queen's accession on 17 November 1595 probably closed his active career, for in 1596 in a letter to Burleigh he lamented his 'long sickness', and in November of that year he was dead.

The versatile talents of Robert Greene achieved nothing of such enduring interest as those autobiographical prose tracts, in which, with some imaginative embroidery, he told the story of his recklessly Bohemian career. In one of these, his *Repentance*, he tells that he was born (probably in 1558) and bred in the city of Norwich, of honest and grave parents, to whose 'wholesome advertisements' he gave a deaf ear. At the University of Cambridge, where he matriculated at St. John's College in 1575, he mis-spent his time 'among wags as lewd as my selfe'. Yet he took his B.A. in 1578, and M.A. in 1583, with a period of foreign travel some time between in Italy and Spain, 'in which places I sawe and practizde such villainie as is abominable to declare'. He was probably back in London in 1580, when the first Part of his *Mamillia, a Mirror or Looking Glass for the Ladies of England*, was entered in the Stationers' Register. As the title suggests, it was a novel in the Euphuistic manner. It was followed by the second Part, entered in 1583, and by a series of similar romances, to some of which were prefixed racy introductory epistles from his or other hands, including his attack in 'an address to the gentlemen readers' prefixed to *Perimedes* (1588) on 'that Atheist *Tamburlan*'.

Greene's account in his *Groatsworth of Wit* of how he began to write for the theatre has already been quoted, but, so far as his extant plays furnish any evidence, it would seem as if it was in emulation of Marlowe's success that he turned his attention to the stage. *Alphonsus, King of Arragon*, written for Lord Strange's men, is an extravagant imitation of *Tamburlaine*, detailing the exploits of a conquering hero, with an astonishing disregard for chronology. Though not published till 1599, it was probably produced about 1588 while *Tamburlaine* was in the high tide of its success, and under the immediate influence of its 'high astounding terms'. *Orlando Furioso* also bears, though in a less pronounced degree, the stamp of *Tamburlaine*. Published in 1594, 'as it was plaid before the Queenes Maiestie', it had been acted by Lord Strange's men on 22 February 1591/2. The choice of a subject from Ariosto's epic was probably suggested to Greene by the appearance in 1591 of Sir John Harington's English translation. But as in Act II. Sc. i, he quotes eight lines from Canto XXVII in Italian, he seems to have used the original text. In any case, in his treatment of the rivalry between Orlando and Sacripant for the love of Angelica, and in other details of the plot, he takes the utmost licence with his source.

But we probably cannot do the play full justice in the 1594 text. There has been preserved at Dulwich, among the Henslowe papers, the 'part' of Orlando, with corrections in the hand of Edward Alleyn who doubtless acted it. A comparison of this 'part' with the corresponding portions of the quarto indicates that the latter is a much abridged version, with some characters omitted, for performance by a reduced cast, probably on a provincial tour.

It has been confidently held by more than one editor of *Friar Bacon and Friar Bungay* that in it also Greene was seeking to rival Marlowe and that the play was written to challenge the resounding success of *Doctor Faustus*. But though not published till 1594 *Friar Bacon and Friar Bungay* was acted, not as a new play, as we know from Henslowe's *Diary*, on 19 February 1591/2. Therefore if *Doctor Faustus*, as seems probable for reasons given above, was not written till later in that year, it followed Greene's play and could not have inspired it. The subject of conjuring, as is evident also from *The Old Wives' Tale*, was very much in the air at this time, and just as Marlowe made use of the English *Faust Book*, so did Greene of a prose romance *The Famous Historie of Fryer Bacon . . . With the Liues and Deaths of the two Conjurers, Bungye and Vandermast*. But Greene treats his source with greater freedom than Marlowe. He presents Bacon first in his 'secret cell' in Brasenose College, Oxford, making boast of his powers to three Doctors of the University:

> The great arch-ruler, potentate of hell,
> Trembles when Bacon bids him, or his fiends,
> Bow to the force of his Pentageron.
> . . . .
> I have contrived and framed a head of brass
> (I made Belcephon hammer out the stuff),
> And that by art shall read philosophy.

When one of the Doctors incredulously declares that 'this is a fable Aesop had forgot', Bacon gives a proof of his powers that puts him to shame.

But the Friar soon has more illustrious visitors. From a mere hint in the *Historie* Greene brings not only King

Henry III, but the German Emperor and the King of Castile, with his daughter Elinor, on an entirely unhistorical visit to Oxford to witness a trial of their arts between Bacon and Bungay and the German Vandermast in the Emperor's train. It is pleasant to find the Cantab, Greene, putting into the mouth of the Emperor a eulogy of Oxford, though the mention of 'mountains' scarcely points to first-hand observation (III. ii):

> Trust me, Plantagenet, these Oxford schools
> Are richly seated near the river side:
> The mountains full of fat and fallow deer,
> The battelling[1] pastures laid[2] with kine or flocks,
> The town gorgeous with high built colleges,
> And scholars seemly in their grave attire,
> Learned in searching principles of art.

The scene that follows in which the English conjurers worst the German is taken from the *Historie* as is also that (IV. i) in which the Brazen Head speaks thrice the curt words, 'Time is', 'Time was', 'Time is past', while Bacon and Bungay lie sleeping after sixty days of toil. Bacon's 'poor scholar', Miles, who has been set to keep watch does not think it worth while to wake his master to hear such utterances till the Brazen Head is broken in pieces, and Bacon's 'seven years' study lieth in the dust'. Yet Miles, with his scraps of verse after the manner of Skelton, has been such an amusing rogue that we could wish him a less drastic penalty for his negligence than to be carried off 'roaring' to hell on a devil's back.

Bacon has still command, however, of his 'glass perspective', and with it in another scene (IV. iii) borrowed from the *Historie* he shows two young scholars a vision of their fathers engaged in a fatal affray, whereupon they stab each other to death. In horror Bacon breaks

[1] fattening. [2] laden.

his glass, and vows to spend the remnant of his life in pure devotion. Yet he retains enough of his art to be able to prophesy, in compliment to the Virgin Queen, that from the marriage of Elinor of Castile with Prince Edward, which closes the play, there will spring in time a matchless flower, Diana's rose, to 'overshadow Albion with her leaves'. But Prince Edward has been no fervent wooer. With the rivalry between the conjurers Greene has deftly interwoven an underplot of love-rivalry for Margaret, the fair maid of Fresingfield. It is an idyll of East Anglia, Greene's native district, in which the heir to the throne falls a victim to the rustic charms of a keeper's daughter, who gives her heart to his proxy wooer, the Earl of Lincoln. Edward takes a strange way to the affections of a country lass when he tells her (III. i):

> Like Thetis shalt thou wanton on the waves,
> And draw the dolphins to thy lovely eyes,
> To dance lavoltas in the purple streams.
> Sirens, with harps and silver psalteries,
> Shall wait with music at thy frigate's stem,
> And entertain fair Margaret with their lays.

And Margaret is scarcely less 'highbrow' in her thanks to the prince when at last he surrenders her to his favoured rival:

> Then lordly sir, whose conquest is as great
> In conquering love, as Caesar's victories,
> Margaret, as mild and humble in her thoughts
> As was Aspasia unto Cyrus' self
> Yields thanks, and next lord Lacy, doth enshrine
> Edward the second secret in her heart.

Yet, in spite of her far-fetched similes, the keeper's daughter is a warm-hearted and simple village maid.

Attractive types of loyal womanhood in loftier social

spheres are drawn by Greene in *The Scottish History of James the Fourth.* It was entered in the Stationers' Register on 14 May 1594, and published in 1598. The considerable proportion of rhymed verse in the play seems to point to the diminishing influence of Marlowe on Greene's style, and favours a late date, about 1591. In spite of the title there is singularly little 'Scottish History' in *James the Fourth*, which is based, with an almost complete change of names upon an Italian novel by Giraldi Cinthio. The novel did not contain any of the supernatural features which had an attraction for Greene, but he introduces them in a curious kind of chorus, which has two chief figures, Oberon, King of Fairies, and a cynical Scot, Bohan, to whom Oberon exhibits dancing 'Antiques' and various dumb shows. When Bohan, in Greene's attempt at Scottish vernacular, cries, 'Thou wilt not threap[1] me, this whiniard[2] has gard[3] many better men to lope[4] then thou', the Fairy King lays a charm upon his sword. Thereafter the cynic presents the main story in action before Oberon that he may 'judge if any wise man would not leave the world if he could'.

Yet such misanthropy does not find justification in what follows. King James is indeed an unfaithful husband, and in his determination to gratify his guilty passion for Ida, daughter of the Countess of Arran, even connives at the attempted murder of his queen, the English princess Dorothea. His main instrument is the Machiavellian villain Ateukin, who expounds a more than Stuart doctrine of the divine right of Kings:

> You have the sword and sceptre in your hand;
> You are the king, the state depends on you;
> Your will is law.

[1] Contradict. [2] Short sword. [3] Made. [4] Leap.

But in glowing contrast are the chaste resolutions of Ida, who repels all the advances of her royal wooer, and the tender constancy of Dorothea, who, though driven from Court in page's disguise and wounded by a hired assassin, does not waver in her wedded love till she is reunited with James. As Churton Collins in his Oxford edition of the dramatist has truly said, 'there is one type of woman of which all Greene's best female characters are repetitions, and Dorothea is their queen, the crown and flower of them'.

Apart from other plays, including the attractive *George-a-Greene, the Pinner of Wakefield*, which have been attributed to him on more or less doubtful grounds, Greene, as the title-page informs us, was joint-author with Thomas Lodge of *A Looking Glass for London and England* (published 1594). Lodge, a son of a Lord Mayor of London, was born in 1557 or 1558 and was educated at Merchant Taylors', Trinity College, Oxford, where he graduated in 1577, and Lincoln's Inn. He began literary life as a pamphleteer and novelist, and in 1588 took part in an expedition to the Canaries. During this voyage he wrote his Euphuistic romance, *Rosalynde*, the source of *As You Like It*. And it was probably before he undertook another, more ill-starred, voyage with Cavendish in 1591 that he collaborated with Greene in *A Looking-Glass*. As Lodge's name appears first on the title-page, and as two scenes are based on his pamphlet *An Alarum against Usurers* (1584) and others have echoes of his marine experiences, he appears to have had the main share of the work. The lighter prose scenes, of which an amusing clown is the centre, are in Greene's less serious vein, though the play as a whole breathes the spirit of his 'repentance' pamphlets. Rasni, King of Nineveh, the conqueror of Jeroboam, is portrayed, evidently after the model of Tamburlaine, as an oriental despot intoxicated with boundless power:

> My sceptre straineth both the parallels.

His court and capital seethe with vice and oppression till the preaching of 'Jonas' suddenly brings about repentance and reformation. Here is a looking-glass in which, as the prophet warns the audience in the theatre, 'you islanders' may see themselves, and London, in which are 'more sins than Nineveh contains', may wake from her blindness and turn weeping to the Lord.

In the same year as *The Looking Glass* (1594) Lodge published a play entirely from his own pen, *The Wounds of Civil War*. It dealt with 'the true tragedies' of Marius and Sulla, and is notable as one of the few extant dramas previous to those of Shakespeare and Jonson, based on the history of Rome. But that history is strangely fantasticated when Sulla appears in triumph with his chariot, after the fashion of Tamburlaine, drawn by four Moors, or when the Gaul who has been sent to kill Marius in prison cries terror-stricken in French 'as she is spoke', 'Adieu, Messieurs; me be dead si je touche Marius . . . Marius est diable. Jesu Maria, sava moy'. The play, which has touches of Roman vigour, had in part a propagandist aim. As the lawyers of the Inner Temple had in 1562 exemplified from legendary British history in *Gorboduc* the 'wounds of civil war',[1] so some thirty years later the Lord Admiral's company, in Lodge's play, brought the same lesson home on the professional stage from the annals of republican Rome.

[1] See above, pp. 32–3.

Thomas Nashe, born at Lowestoft in 1567, was, like Greene, an East Anglian, and followed him to St. John's College, Cambridge, in 1582, graduating in 1586, and coming up to London about 1588. His first publication, the epistle prefixed to Greene's novel *Menaphon* (1589), from which the probable reference to Kyd has been quoted, was severely critical of a number of contemporary actors and dramatists. Thus began the long campaign of controversial pamphleteering which he carried on with astounding zest and pungency. Greene in his *Groatsworth of Wit* almost certainly speaks of him as 'young Juvenal, that biting satirist, that lastly with me together writ a comedy'. Nothing further, however, is known of this, and, as has been seen, there is little trace, except on the title-page, of Nashe's collaboration with Marlowe in *Dido*. According to his own account he wrote only the Induction and the first Act of *The Isle of Dogs*, a play which came under the ban of the Privy Council, in the summer of 1597, apparently for some indiscreet reference to foreign affairs. Nashe, to escape arrest, had to take flight to Great Yarmouth, and probably wrote no more plays during the years before his death, which is mentioned in 1601. Thus the only extant dramatic piece which can be ascribed entirely to Nashe is *Summer's Last Will and Testament* (published 1600). It is of an allegorical type. Owing to the ravages of plague 'in this latter end of Summer', Summer comes in sick to yield his throne to Autumn. The Seasons appear in turn, with their offspring and companions, such as Orion, Harvest, and Christmas. Within the conventional framework Nashe is able to exhibit his characteristic mastery of phrase, and to pay compliments to the Queen who was at the time on progress. Songs are sung by boys, and Will Summer, Henry VIII's fool, whose name lent itself to the purpose, plays the part of a chorus.

From internal allusions the piece appears to have been acted in 1592 in the house and presence of a Lord, also called 'your grace', at Croydon. This can scarcely be other than the palace of Archbishop Whitgift, whose household may have been the actors. What a singular sidelight have we here on the continuity, amidst all changes, of Tudor drama! We took as its starting-point in Chapter I Medwall's *Fulgens and Lucres*, written when he was chaplain to the Cardinal Archbishop Morton and probably performed in his palace at Lambeth. Wellnigh a century had since gone by and an Anglican instead of a Roman Catholic Archbishop now sat in the seat of Augustine. But at Croydon under Whitgift, as at Lambeth under Morton, drama was fostered and welcomed. The Puritan cleavage between stage and church was still in the future. And, paradoxically, while Medwall about 1497 was beginning the era of English secular drama, Nashe in 1592 was giving a fresh turn to the antiquated allegorical type. Through all the developments and experiments briefly traced in this *Introduction* elements survived from the days of the *Miracle* and the *Morality*. Nor did the death of the Virgin Queen in 1603 bring an abrupt change. The title 'Elizabethan' is still conveniently used to cover the whole range of drama till the outbreak of the Civil War. But the playwrights who began their career in the last years of Elizabeth's reign—Ben Jonson, Dekker, Marston, Chapman, Thomas Heywood, and even, though somewhat their senior, Shakespeare himself—continued and completed their work in a subtly changed atmosphere, under the influence of a semi-foreign King and a foreign Queen. The century of Tudor drama was at an end.

INDEX